Quality Time Anytime!

How to Make the Most of Every Moment with Your Child

Penny Warner

Meadowbrook Press
Distributed by Simon & Schuster
New York

Library of Congress Cataloging-in-Publication Data
Warner, Penny.
Quality time anytime: 200 activities to make the most of every moment with your child / by Penny Warner.
p.cm
ISBN 0-88166-425-1
1. Family recreation. 2. Parent and child. 3. Child development. I. Title.
GV182.8 .W37 2002
796–dc21
2002066009

Editorial Director: Christine Zuchora-Walske
Editor: Joseph Gredler
Proofreader: Megan McGinnis
Production Manager: Paul Woods
Art Director: Peggy Bates
Desktop Publishing: Heather Kern
Illustrator: Susan Spellman
Cover Photos: Ariel Skelly and Jose L. Pelaez, Corbis-Stock Market

Published by: Meadowbrook Press
5451 Smetana Drive
Minnetonka, Minnesota 55343

www.meadowbrookpress.com

BOOK TRADE DISTRIBUTION by Simon & Schuster, a division of Simon and Schuster, Inc., 1230 Avenue of the Americas, New York, New York 10020

06 05 04 03 02 9 8 7 6 5 4 3 2 1

Printed in the United States of America

Dedication

To Tom, Matt, and Rebecca:
Thanks for sharing your quality time with me.

Contents

Introduction

The time you spend with your child is precious. As any parent of a grown child will tell you, time flies by much too quickly. Looking back, most parents think, "I wish I'd spent more time with my kids." Avoid this unfortunate realization by not focusing too much attention on other responsibilities. Instead, step back and enjoy what's really important: quality time with your child.

What Is Quality Time?

Development experts have written a lot about *quality time*. The term was created when experts found that parents were too busy working, taking care of the house, running errands, and doing other jobs to spend much worthwhile time with their kids. Many parents began scheduling time with their children in order to spend meaningful moments with their fast-growing young ones.

Why Quality Time *Anytime?*

Since then we've learned that quality time can be anytime. There are many times throughout the day (standing in line, waiting for the doctor, driving the kids to school, getting ready for bed, and so on) when we fritter away opportunities to have fun with our children. We could easily turn these situations into quality time filled with intellectual challenges, physical tasks, sensory stimulation, and just plain fun.

All it takes is a little imagination, a few supplies, and the hundreds of ideas found in this book. You'll discover games and activities to help you enjoy unplanned moments with your child—even on days when your schedule is packed. In addition, you'll find even more ideas when you check out the "Next Time" section at the end of each activity. There's no end to the fun you can have throughout the day no matter where you are or what you're doing.

The goal of *Quality Time Anytime* is to help you raise a happy, confident, responsible, child who thinks creatively, solves problems, enjoys social interaction, and has good physical skills. Not only will your child learn the crucial skills that will serve her the rest of her life, the activities in *Quality Time Anytime* will also enhance your special bond with her.

Core Values

While your child is enjoying the fun, she'll also be learning these core values:

- **Achievement/Success:** striving for excellence and accomplishing something.
- **Courage:** trying new things and not being afraid to experiment.
- **Curiosity:** questioning, exploring, and accepting challenges that lead to discovery and knowledge.
- **Emotional Expression:** learning the importance of expressing herself and understanding her wide range of emotions.
- **Environmental Awareness:** being aware of her surroundings (home, neighborhood, community, what's in front of her) and doing her part to improve things.
- **Helping Others:** lending her assistance when family and friends need help.
- **Honesty:** being truthful with herself and others.
- **Importance of Family:** understanding why her family is important to her—and her to them.
- **Morals and Beliefs:** learning moral behavior and the beliefs her family shares.
- **Perseverance:** not giving up easily; trying until she's successful.
- **Positive Attitude:** believing she can do something and maintaining an optimistic attitude while trying to meet her goals.
- **Resourcefulness:** coming up with new ways to solve problems.

- **Respect for Nature:** knowing her environment and how she can help keep it thriving.
- **Respect for Others:** learning empathy for others and how to treat them with respect.
- **Responsibility:** knowing when something is important and taking care of her responsibilities.
- **Self-Confidence:** believing in herself and knowing she's competent.
- **Self-Reliance:** trusting in herself and believing she can take care of herself.
- **Self-Respect/Self-Esteem/Self-Awareness:** knowing that it's okay to be herself, learning to accept herself the way she is, and having a sense of her uniqueness.
- **Sense of Humor:** seeing the humor in life and being able to laugh at herself, even when things aren't going according to plan.
- **Setting Goals:** breaking a larger challenge into smaller tasks and taking meaningful steps as she strives to achieve a goal.
- **Teamwork:** cooperating with others and working together to accomplish something.

Basic Skills

Your child will also be enhancing these basic skills:

- **Classification:** organizing his world by classifying objects according to common traits.
- **Communication:** communicating with others using speech, body language, facial expressions, writing, and drama.
- **Coordination/Balance:** using perceptual abilities and muscle groups to maintain body positions.
- **Cooking:** using utensils, appliances, and recipes to create snacks, meals, and other concoctions.

- **Creativity and Imagination:** thinking "outside the box," trying new ideas, creating solutions, and solving problems.
- **Critical Thinking:** analyzing a situation and attempting a solution.
- **Fine Motor:** using fingers and hands to accomplish physical tasks.
- **Following Directions:** understanding, remembering, and following oral or written instructions.
- **Gross Motor:** using arms, legs, and body to accomplish physical tasks.
- **Language and Vocabulary:** increasing vocabulary and language skills for better communication and thought.
- **Manners:** being polite, using good manners, and understanding the importance of appropriate social behavior.
- **Map Reading:** reading, understanding, and following a map; following directions and locating a destination.
- **Math:** using basic number skills such as addition, subtraction, and multiplication as well as more advanced arithmetic.
- **Measuring:** learning to measure in a variety of ways including volume, length, amount, and so on.
- **Memory:** recalling past experiences and information and using them when needed.
- **Perception:** seeing the world clearly and in new ways; evaluating and analyzing what he perceives.
- **Planning/Scheduling:** developing a coherent idea of what's needed to accomplish a task; managing his time efficiently.
- **Practical:** using basic skills needed in daily life, such as bed making, table setting, room cleaning, and so on.
- **Problem Solving:** analyzing a situation and brainstorming solutions.
- **Productivity:** creating a finished product.
- **Recycling:** turning discarded materials into useful products, reusing objects, and helping preserve the environment.

- **Scientific Analysis:** using scientific techniques to analyze a problem.
- **Social Interaction:** communicating with people and appreciating the importance of helping one another.
- **Value of Money:** understanding the value of money and how to earn it.

Teachable Moments

Teachable moments are opportunities that allow you to instruct your child in a positive way. You encourage your child to practice important skills, learn new ways of thinking, and explore her feelings while having fun. It's important to emphasize the *process* rather than the *product*.

The "learn by doing" activities in *Quality Time Anytime* will help your child apply her new knowledge and skills to tasks she'll perform throughout her life. Every moment in your child's life is essentially a teachable moment—an opportunity for her to learn something. Whether you introduce a new skill, a new belief, a new thought, or a new way of looking at things, it only takes a few minutes to have quality time with your child.

Time for Fun

The ultimate goal of *Quality Time Anytime* is fun for you and your child. I've organized the activities into thirteen common situations most families encounter throughout the day—times when you can have fun with your child.

- **Bath Time:** Have fun in the tub while your child gets clean.
- **Bedroom Time:** Enjoy your child's special space together.
- **Bedtime:** Ease your child into bed as he winds down for sleep.
- **Car Time:** Enjoy traveling around town or on long trips.
- **Kitchen Time:** Have some kitchen fun while you cook.

- **Mealtime:** Enjoy your time at the table with your loved ones.
- **Outdoor Time:** Enjoy the great outdoors and its unlimited possibilities.
- **Play Time:** Enjoy fun time and learning time, too.
- **Quiet Time:** Have fun even when it's time to be quiet.
- **Shopping Time:** Keep your child occupied while you do your shopping.
- **Sick Time:** Cheer up your sick child with play-in-bed activities.
- **Waiting Time:** Make time fly with while-you-wait fun.
- **Walking Time:** Discover fresh-air fun as you walk to school, the park, or around the neighborhood.

Format for Fun

Each of the thirteen chapters offers approximately fifteen games and activities created specifically for short periods of time throughout the day. Each section contains the following:

- **Ages:** range of ages appropriate for the activity.
- **Introduction:** brief explanation of the game or activity.
- **Values and Skills:** lists of the values and skills your child will learn while engaged in the activity.
- **Materials:** list of props necessary to carry out the activity.
- **How to Play:** easy step-by-step instructions.
- **Next Time:** suggestions for extending the fun.

Chapter One

Bath Time!

Ages: 2 to 4 years

Fizzy Water

Plop! Plop! Fizz! Fizz! Oh, what a fun bath it is! Can your child figure out why it's so fizzy?

Values
- Resourcefulness

Skills
- Critical Thinking

Materials
- Alka-Seltzer or effervescent bath tablets

How to Play
1. Fill the bathtub with warm water and have your child hop in.
2. Drop a tablet or two into the water behind your child's back so she can't see it.
3. Ask her if she feels anything in the water.
4. Ask her to describe the feeling and the sound.
5. Have her look for the source of the fizzies.
6. See if she can guess what it is and why it fizzes.
7. Explain to her how the ingredients in the tablet react with the water to create the fizzing.
8. See if she can think of other things that might cause a fizzing or bubbling reaction in the water.

Next Time
- Try other products that fizz or dissolve, such as bath salts, bubble bath, and so on.
- See if you can make other products react when combined, such as vinegar and baking soda, soda water and ice cream, and so on.

Ages: 3 to 8 years

Hair Salon

Your child can go to the hair salon every time he takes a bath! Create the wildest hairdos ever imagined!

Values
- Self-Awareness

Skills
- Creativity and Imagination

Materials
- Nonbreakable mirror
- Children's shampoo (lathering)
- Camera (optional)

How to Play
1. Fill the tub with warm water and have your child hop in.
2. Place a nonbreakable mirror near the tub so your child can see himself.
3. Apply shampoo to your child's hair and work up a lather.
4. Encourage him to create wild and crazy hairstyles with the shampoo.
5. Have him look in the mirror to see the results.
6. Take photos to preserve the memories, if desired.

Next Time
- Use a little food coloring in the shampoo to create colorful hairstyles. (The color will wash out.)
- Help your child create even more exotic hairstyles by giving him props such as chopsticks, big-tooth combs, hair clips, and so on.

Ages: 3 to 6 years

How Many Cups?

Have your child guess how many cups of water it takes to fill a container. It's harder than it looks!

Values
- Curiosity

Skills
- Math

Materials
- Plastic measuring cups
- Containers of different sizes

How to Play
1. Fill the tub with warm water and have your child hop in.
2. Place plastic measuring cups and containers in the water.
3. Fill one large container with water.
4. Ask your child to guess how many cups of water are in the container.
5. To check the answer, have her measure the amount of water using the measuring cups.
6. Repeat using other containers and measuring cups.

Next Time
- Use teaspoons and small cups to measure the water.
- Use other items to measure with, such as a baster, plastic bottle, plastic bowl, washcloth or sponge (fill, then squeeze), and so on.
- Add different food colorings to the various containers of water.

Ages: 3 to 6 years

Missing Money

Money doesn't grow on trees, but your child might find some at the bottom of the bathtub!

Values
- Perseverance

Skills
- Fine Motor

Materials
- Five to ten pennies or other small coins

How to Play
1. Fill the tub with warm water and have your child hop in.
2. Count out five to ten pennies.
3. Have your child listen with his eyes closed as you toss one coin into the water.
4. Have him try to find the coin by remembering where he heard it land.
5. Repeat with the other coins.

Next Time
- Throw several coins in the water one by one, and have your child try to find them by remembering where he heard them land.
- Add more coins each time you play.
- Toss other sinking objects into the water one by one, and have your child guess what the objects are by listening to them hit the water. Then have him retrieve the objects.

Sing a Duet

You've heard how good your singing sounds in the shower. Try singing a duet with your child in the bathtub for a great new sound.

Values
- Teamwork

Skills
- Following Directions
- Memory

Materials
- Your voices

How to Play

1. Fill the tub with warm water and have your child hop in.
2. Ask our child to start singing "Row, row, row, your boat...."
3. As he sings "Merrily, merrily...," you start singing "Row, row, row, your boat."

Next Time
- Pick another favorite song. ("You Are My Sunshine" offers a good opportunity to try out your skill with harmony.)

Ages: 3 to 8 years

Sink the Ship

It doesn't take loose lips to sink ships—it takes too much weight! Can your child guess how much?

Values
- Perseverance

Skills
- Critical Thinking
- Fine Motor

Materials
- Flat plastic boat or flat piece of wood
- Small objects to put on the boat, such as toothpaste caps, Q-Tips, spools, small toys, nail clippers, and so on

How to Play
1. Fill the tub with warm water and have your child hop in.
2. Set the boat or piece of wood on top of the water.
3. Drop small objects into the water or set them nearby.
4. Have your child guess how many objects the boat will hold before it sinks.
5. Have her test her hypothesis to see how successful she is.

Next Time
- Choose different objects and try again.
- Set the items on the boat in a different order to see if that makes a difference.
- Try different boats.
- Use all the same objects.

Ages: 5 to 8 years

Slow Motion

Once your child learns a simple task like putting on a sock, it's easy to do—unless water makes him move in slow motion!

Values
- Resourcefulness

Skills
- Fine Motor

Materials
- Old sock or scarf

How to Play
1. Fill the tub with warm water and have your child hop in.
2. Choose a simple task such as putting on a sock or tying a scarf into a bow.
3. Put one of the objects in the water.
4. Have your child try to perform the task with the object underwater.

Next Time
- Give your child other tasks to perform, such as buttoning a shirt, dressing a baby doll, or doing a plastic puzzle underwater.

Ages: 3 to 8 years

Sponge Shapes

Does your child know that your bathtub acts as a magical magnet when it gets wet? Have her try it and see what sticks!

Values
- Curiosity

Skills
- Scientific Analysis

Materials
- Clean sponges cut into a variety of shapes
- Other objects that may stick to the tub when wet, such as balloons, waxed paper, fabric, plastic bookmarks, and so on

How to Play
1. Fill the tub with warm water and have your child hop in.
2. Cut the sponges into a variety of shapes.
3. Drop the sponges into the water.
4. Have your child arrange the sponges into a design by pressing them against the wall of the tub.
5. See how long the sponges stay up. Have her create new designs after they fall.

Next Time
- Cut the sponges into alphabet shapes.
- Have your child guess what else will stick to the wall of the tub. Have her try it out.

Ages: 5 to 8 years

Sticker Magic

Have your child create his own bathtub funnies!

Values
- Resourcefulness

Skills
- Creativity and Imagination

Materials
- Comic strips from books or newspapers
- Clear Contact paper
- Scissors

How to Play
1. Cut comic strips into individual squares.
2. Cut a sheet of clear Contact paper big enough to cover all the squares.
3. Peel off the backing and place the squares one inch apart on the sticky side of the Contact paper.
4. Place another sheet of Contact paper on top of the squares.
5. Cut out the individual squares, leaving a small border around each square to keep it sealed.
6. Fill the tub full of warm water and have your child hop in.
7. Place the comic squares nearby or float them on the water.
8. Have your child create a story by choosing squares and arranging them on the wall of the tub.

Next Time
- Have your child draw his own cartoons. Cover them with Contact paper and use them as described above.

Ages: 4 to 8 years

Take It with Tongs

Picking up things with your fingers is easy for your child. Picking up things with tongs is not—especially if the items are in water!

Values
- Perseverance

Skills
- Fine Motor

Materials
- Small objects that float, such as toothpaste caps, Q-Tips, small combs, hair bands, plastic spoons, and so on
- Tongs

How to Play
1. Fill the tub with warm water and have your child hop in.
2. Drop the objects in the water.
3. Have your child try to pick them up with the tongs.

Next Time
- Choose different objects each time you play.
- Choose smaller objects to make it more challenging.
- See if your child can pick up two items at the same time.
- Have your child try picking up objects with chopsticks.

Ages: 3 to 6 years

Tea for Two in the Tub

Has your child ever had a tea party in the bathtub? It's the perfect place to pour without worrying about spilling!

Values
- Importance of Family

Skills
- Social Interaction

Materials
- Plastic tea set
- Piece of wood to float on the water as a table (for example, a cutting board)

How to Play
1. Fill the tub with warm water and have your child hop in.
2. Float a piece of wood on the water to serve as a table.
3. Place the plastic tea set on the edge of the tub or in the water.
4. Have your child "set the table" and fill the cups with "tea."
5. Enjoy a conversation while you "sip" your tea.

Next Time
- Color the teapot water with food coloring before your child pours it into the teacups.
- Serve lemonade or juice in the teapot.

Ages: 3 to 8 years

Tub Art

Art is where you find it—even in the bathtub! All your child needs are some supplies to shape a masterpiece.

Values

- Emotional Expression

Skills

- Creativity and Imagination

Materials

- Shaving cream
- Plastic bowl
- Food coloring
- Mirror (optional)

How to Play

1. Fill the tub half full with warm water and have your child hop in.
2. Squirt a small amount of shaving cream into a plastic bowl.
3. Tint the shaving cream with a little food coloring.
4. Let your child "shape" a picture on the inside wall of the tub with the colored shaving cream.
5. When she's finished with her picture, rinse it off and start again.

Next Time

- Tint several bowls of shaving cream in a variety of colors so your child can create a multicolored picture.
- Provide a mirror and let your child dot the shaving cream on her face and body. Make sure she's careful not to get it in her eyes.

Ages: 3 to 8 years

Water Science

The bathtub is a fascinating scientific laboratory. Have your child try a few experiments and see what happens!

Values
- Environmental Awareness

Skills
- Scientific Analysis

Materials
- "Science" toys such as measuring cups, basters, nesting cups, a magnifying glass, a sieve, and so on

How to Play
1. Fill the tub with warm water and have your child hop in.
2. Place several "science" toys in the water.
3. Let your child experiment with the objects and figure out what they can do. Suggest a few experiments if she needs help. For example, she might see how many measuring cups it takes to fill another container, see how far she can squirt water from a baster, look underwater with a magnifying glass, see if she can collect water in a sieve, see how many small objects she can pick up with the sieve, and so on.
4. Ask your child to explain the experiments she performs.

Next Time
- Provide different objects to experiment with.
- Have her do sink-or-float experiments using various items.

Water Toss

Can your child toss an object into a bowl? Sounds easy, unless the bowl is moving!

Values
- Achievement/Success

Skills
- Perception

Materials
- Small plastic bowl
- Small plastic caps, poker chips, coins, dice, or other small objects

How to Play
1. Fill the tub with warm water and have your child hop in.
2. Float the bowl on top of the water.
3. Have your child try to toss small objects into the bowl.

Next Time
- Have him try tossing with his eyes closed.
- Choose a smaller bowl.
- Make waves in the water to keep the bowl moving.

Chapter Two

Bedroom Time!

Ages: 8 to 12 years

Doorknob Signs

Help your child communicate her feelings with doorknob signs.

Values
- Emotional Expression

Skills
- Communication

Materials
- Scissors
- Stiff poster board in a variety of colors
- String, markers
- Stickers or drawings

How to Play
1. Cut poster board of various colors into 4-by-8-inch rectangles. Choose colors that signify certain emotions, such as blue for sad.
2. Cut holes near the top of each rectangle so you can tie a piece of string for hanging over a doorknob.
3. Have your child write a phrase that matches the color/emotion, such as "Boo-hoo. I'm blue," or "Not mad or glad. Just sad."
4. Have her add stickers or drawings to match the emotions.
5. Make a whole set of doorknob signs to indicate various emotions.
6. Have your child hang the appropriate one on her doorknob each day. She can change the sign as her feelings change.

Next Time
- Have your child make doorknob signs to tell others what she's doing, where she's been, and so on.
- Have her draw faces on poster board and hang them on the door.

Hooray
Let's Play!

Ages: 6 to 10 years

Fashion Disaster

Many kids try to coordinate their outfits, but can your child be the one to mismatch the most?

Values
- Sense of Humor

Skills
- Creativity and Imagination

Materials
- Clothes from your child's wardrobe
- Camera (optional)

How to Play
1. Have your child select mismatching items from her closet and drawers.
2. Have her put together the wildest outfit she can.
3. Play the game with family and friends and see who can create the most bizarre outfit.
4. If desired, take photos so you can remember the moment.

Next Time
- Have her put on another person's clothes to create a crazy outfit.
- Supplement the outfit with wild items from a thrift shop.

Ages: 8 to 12 years

Goalie

Have your child set goals, make a chart, and hang it in his room so he can watch his progress each day.

Values
- Responsibility
- Setting Goals

Skills
- Planning/Scheduling

Materials
- Markers
- Large sheet of poster board

How to Play
1. Have your child think of three goals he'd like to achieve, such as "Turn in my math homework on time," "Make my bed every day," and "Talk to one new kid at school each week."
2. Have him write down his goals on the poster board. Together, choose an appropriate reward for meeting them.
3. Have him make a calendar grid to mark off the days until he meets his goals.
4. Hang up the chart so he can see it every day.
5. Have him mark his progress daily in the appropriate box.
6. Reward him with a prize when he reaches his goals.

Next Time
- Have your child make a chore chart so he can check off each item as he completes it each day.

Ages: 4 to 8 years

Office Hours

Have your child turn her bedroom into an executive office and go to work just like her parents!

Values
- Self-Reliance

Skills
- Critical Thinking

Materials
- Desk (real or makeshift)
- Paper and pencils
- Supplies such as a coffee mug, bag lunch, note pad, and so on
- Computer or typewriter (toy, new, or used)
- Toy telephone or unplugged real phone

How to Play
1. Have your child use her imagination to set up an office in her bedroom.
2. Help her create a desk using an old table, or make one from cardboard.
3. Supply her office with paper, pencils, and so on.
4. Let your child enjoy her day at the office by typing up information, having meetings, making phone calls, setting goals for her company, and so on.

Next Time
- Have her set up a hospital, post office, cruise ship, school, or anything else she might enjoy.

Ages: 6 to 10 years

Outlines

If your child thinks she knows the objects in her room well, have her try to draw them from memory.

Values
- Environmental Awareness

Skills
- Memory

Materials
- Paper and pencil

How to Play
1. Have your child choose an object in her room.
2. Have her draw an outline of it and show it to you.
3. Try to guess what it is.
4. Take turns drawing and guessing objects.

Next Time
- Time yourselves to see how long it takes you to guess correctly.
- Instead of drawing the object, describe it until the other person guesses what it is.

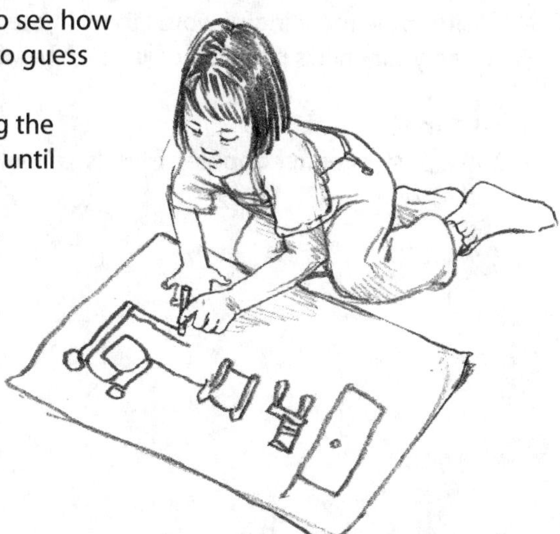

Ages: 4 to 12 years

Personal Collage

Help your child make a personalized poster featuring her favorite mementos!

Values
- Self-Esteem/Self-Awareness

Skills
- Perception

Materials
- Large poster board
- Photographs of your child
- Small mementos
- Scissors, tape or glue, markers

How to Play
1. Have your child select a few of her photos from family albums.
2. Gather some of her special mementos collected over the years.
3. Arrange the items, and tape or glue them onto the poster board.
4. Write some meaningful words to fill in the spaces.
5. Hang your child's personal collage on her bedroom wall.

Next Time
- Make posters of her hobbies, friends, schoolwork, vacations, and so on.

Ages: 7 to 12 years

Pickup Race

How fast can your child clean his room? Have him challenge himself to a race!

Values
- Resourcefulness

Skills
- Practical

Materials
- Stopwatch or watch with a second hand
- Paper and pencil

How to Play
1. Set the stopwatch to zero, or wait until the second hand reaches twelve.
2. Tell your child to clean up his room as quickly as he can.
3. Press start, if necessary, and record the amount of time it takes him to clean his room.
4. Record his times each time you play the game. Challenge him to beat his best time.

Next Time
- Time him getting dressed, walking to school, mowing the lawn, and so on.
- Give him a specific amount of time to complete a task. See if he can do it!

Ages: 3 to 6 years

Pile Up

Can your child stack a tower of toys before they all come tumbling down? See how high she can go!

Values
- Curiosity

Skills
- Fine Motor

Materials
- Several toys or small objects (nonbreakable)

How to Play
1. Find a flat surface to stack on.
2. Collect a bunch of toys that will be fun to stack.
3. Take turns stacking one toy on another.
4. The person who causes the tower to fall loses the game!

Next Time
- Measure the tower's height each time your child plays, and see if she can beat her record.

Ages: 6 to 12 years

Private Arcade

Help your child turn his bedroom into a private arcade with games galore.

Values
- Resourcefulness

Skills
- Fine Motor

Materials
- Objects in your child's room that can be used as targets, such as a wastebasket, book bag, shoebox, action figures, and so on
- Objects in your child's room that can be safely tossed or rolled, such as paper wads, small stuffed animals, marbles, balled socks, and so on

How to Play
1. Set up targets around your child's bedroom. For example, you might set a wastebasket on a chair, hang a book bag from a doorknob, lay a shoebox on its side on the floor, line up action figures along the windowsill, and so on.
2. Help your child gather objects to toss in the center of his room.
3. Sit in the center of the room and try to complete each challenge you've set up. For example, you might try to see how many paper wads you can toss into the wastebasket, how many stuffed animals you can land in the book bag, how many marbles you can roll into the shoebox, and how many action figures you can knock over with the balled socks.

Next Time
- Invent your own bedroom arcade games.
- Have your child invite siblings or friends to his room to test their skills in his arcade.

Ages: 5 to 10 years

Rainbow Clothes

Here's an easy way to help your child organize her clothes. It's fun, easy, and as colorful as the rainbow!

Values
- Self-Reliance

Skills
- Classification

Materials
- Socks in a drawer

How to Play
1. Pull out all your child's socks from the drawer.
2. Have her sort them according to color.
3. Have her put them back in the drawer according to colors of the rainbow (red, orange, yellow, green, blue, and purple).
4. Once in a while, sneak into your child's room and move a pair of socks to the wrong place. See if she notices!

Next Time
- Have her color coordinate her crayons, books, toys, stuffed animals, and so on.

Ages: 6 to 10 years

Room Detective

How well does your child know what's in her room? Have her play detective to find out what doesn't belong.

Values
- Resourcefulness

Skills
- Memory

Materials
- Object that doesn't belong in your child's bedroom, such as a can of food, her dad's hat, her sister's doll, and so on

How to Play
1. Choose an item that doesn't belong in your child's bedroom.
2. Have her close her eyes or leave the room.
3. Hide the item somewhere in her room.
4. Have her hunt for the object.
5. Give her clues if she has trouble finding it.

Next Time
- Remove an important object from your child's room and let her try to figure out what's missing.
- Play detective games in other rooms.

Ages: 3 to 8 years

Sheet Shack

Let your child cover the furniture in his room with sheets to create a whole new look.

Values
- Self-Reliance

Skills
- Creativity and Imagination

Materials
- Bed sheets
- Props such as a flashlight, toys, snacks, and so on

How to Play
1. Gather some bed sheets from the linen closet or laundry room.
2. Have your child drape them over his bed, dresser, chairs, and other pieces of furniture to create a fort, cave, or miniature house.
3. Provide various props for his sheet-covered home so he can stay and play awhile.

Next Time
- Add large cardboard boxes under the sheets to create tunnels, caves, or small rooms.

Ages: 8 to 12 years

Time Line

Instead of keeping a journal, your child can create her own personal time line to keep track of her life as it unfolds.

Values
- Self-Esteem

Skills
- Language and Vocabulary

Materials
- Tape
- Butcher paper or several sheets of construction paper
- Colorful markers

How to Play
1. Tape a length of butcher paper (or several sheets of construction paper) at shoulder level along one wall of your child's bedroom, from corner to corner.
2. Have your child draw a horizontal line along the center of the paper.
3. Have your child draw a mark at the left end of the line and write the date and time of her birth near the mark.
4. Help your child continue recording all the important events of her life on the time line. She might include the date she said her first word, her first day of kindergarten, all her birthday parties, and the dates of vacations.
5. When the time line is up to date, tape another length of paper to the adjoining wall on the right so your child can record the things that happen as she grows.

Next Time
- As you extend your child's time line, you'll probably think of other important past events. Just add them to the timeline as you remember them.

Transformers

Does your child know the objects in his room can be transformed? Let him see how many things they can transform into!

Values
- Resourcefulness

Skills
- Critical Thinking

Materials
- Furniture and other objects in your child's room

How to Play
1. Have your child choose a piece of furniture or an object in his room, such as the bed, lamp, shoebox, and so on.
2. Have him think of ten ways he could transform the object into something else. For example, he might turn the bed into a trampoline, spaceship, table, stage, strange planet, tent, or picnic blanket (using the sheets), and so on.
3. Take turns choosing objects and transforming them.

Next Time
- See how many times he can transform an object before he gets stuck.
- Play the game in another room.

Chapter Three

Bedtime!

Animal Tales

Just as your child's stuffed animals are coming to life and saving the day, your child is falling asleep!

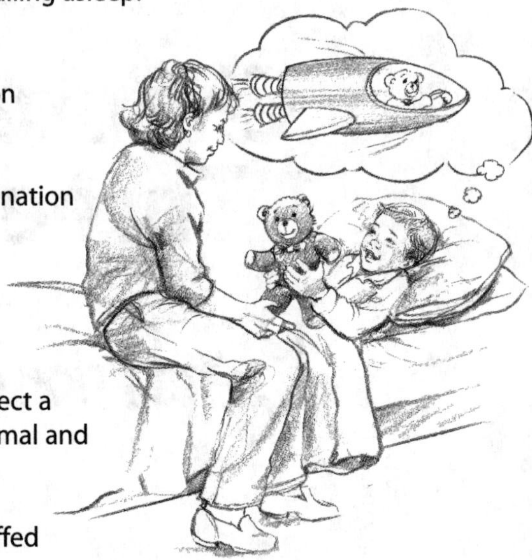

Values
- Emotional Expression

Skills
- Creativity and Imagination

Materials
- Stuffed animals

How to Play
1. Have your child select a favorite stuffed animal and hop into bed.
2. Take turns telling a story using the stuffed animal as the star.
3. Add other animals to the story as you go along.
4. Make sure there's a happy ending so your child can get to sleep!

Next Time
- Choose a different stuffed animal to feature each night.
- Add your child's favorite toys to the story and see what happens.

Ages: 4 to 7 years

Book Cover

Can your child tell a book by its cover? Have him guess what's going to happen before you read the story.

Values
- Resourcefulness

Skills
- Creativity and Imagination
- Language and Vocabulary

Materials
- Children's books (age appropriate)

How to Play
1. Select several library or store-bought books your child hasn't heard or read before.
2. Let him choose one of the books and hop into bed.
3. Have him look at the cover for several minutes and try to figure out what the story is about.
4. Have him make up a story based on the cover.
5. Read the actual story and see if it's similar to the story he made up.

Next Time
- Read the first page and see if your child can guess what's going to happen in the rest of the book.
- Read the last page and see if he can figure out what happens leading up to that point.
- Read one page at a time and see if your child can guess what's going to happen next.

Ages: 4 to 8 years

Draw a Dream

Has your child ever had one of those vivid dreams that seemed almost real? Have her draw a picture of it!

Values
- Self-Esteem/Self-Awareness

Skills
- Creativity and Imagination
- Fine Motor

Materials
- Paper and markers
- Clipboard

How to Play
1. When your child wakes up in the morning or from a nap, see if she can recall one of her dreams.
2. Give her paper, markers, and a clipboard.
3. Have her draw a picture of her dream.
4. Talk about the picture and see if you can tell what it means.

Next Time
- Draw a picture of one of your dreams and see if your child can guess what it means. Don't draw a frightening dream!

Ages: 6 to 12 years

Fight or Flight

What would your child do in a challenging and potentially scary situation? Face his fear—or run away? Find out by playing Fight or Flight.

Values
- Resourcefulness

Skills
- Problem Solving

Materials
- Pencil
- Index cards

How to Play
1. Write down some challenging situations on index cards, such as "What would you do if you saw your neighbor's house on fire?" "What would you do if you were trapped by a big dog?" "What would you do if you were lost in the woods?" (Don't make the questions too scary or your child won't get to sleep!)
2. Have your child hop into bed.
3. Stack the cards and have your child choose one.
4. Read the card to your child and ask him what he'd do in that situation.
5. Brainstorm as many responses as possible, to show your child various options for solving the problem.

Next Time
- Write down crazy questions instead of real ones, such as "What would you do if you went to the moon?" "What would you do if your hair turned purple?" and so on.

Hand Massage

There's nothing like a soothing hand massage to help your child relax and go to sleep.

Values
- Teamwork

Skills
- Social Interaction

Materials
- Hand lotion

How to Play
1. Get some hand lotion and have your child hop into bed.
2. Apply lotion to your hands or your child's hands.
3. Give your child a hand massage.

Next Time
- Have your child give you a hand massage.
- Give each other a foot massage. But watch out! It tickles!

Ages: 4 to 8 years

Happy and You Know It

Have your child look around and find out what makes him happy.

Values
- Emotional Expression

Skills
- Perception

Materials
- Nothing

How to Play
1. Have your child think of something that makes him happy, such as a book, movie, hug, dessert, or gift.
2. Have him talk about why the object or experience makes him happy.
3. Take turns thinking of things that make you happy and talking about them.

Next Time
- Find things that make you feel other emotions such as anger, excitement, and so on.

Ages: 4 to 8 years

Light Chase

Can your child catch the moving light as it races across his bedroom ceiling? He'll have to be fast!

Values
- Teamwork

Skills
- Fine Motor
- Perception

Materials
- Two flashlights

How to Play
1. Get two flashlights and have your child hop into bed.
2. Give him one of the flashlights.
3. Turn off all the lights so the room is dark.
4. Turn on the flashlights and shine them on the ceiling.
5. When you say, "Go," have your child chase your light with his light and see if he can "catch" yours.
6. When he catches yours, reverse the chase.

Next Time
- Move the light around on the ceiling and make up a story to go with the movement. For example, you might move the light across the ceiling, stop it, shake it a little, and say, "Once upon a time there was a firefly who was afraid of the dark." Pass the flashlight to your child and have him continue the story.
- Read a book under the covers using your flashlights.

Ages: 3 to 6 years

Magic Carpet Ride

Your child's bed is the perfect place for her to take a magic carpet ride into her imagination!

Values
- Emotional Expression

Skills
- Creativity and Imagination
- Language and Vocabulary

Materials
- Special blanket or towel

How to Play

1. Spread a special blanket or towel on your child's bed and have her hop on top.
2. Have her close her eyes and imagine that she's sitting on a magic carpet.
3. Ask her to picture where the magic carpet is taking her, and have her describe the trip.
4. Have her talk about what she sees, hears, smells, feels, and experiences.
5. If she gets stuck, give her a prompt such as, "What's in that forest over there?" or "Do you see that unicorn?"

Next Time
- Choose a picture from a book that illustrates an interesting place. Have your child tell a story about the picture.

Ages: 4 to 8 years

Mixed-Up Fairy Tales

What would you get if elements from your child's favorite stories were combined? A crazy, mixed-up fairy tale, that's what!

Values
- Resourcefulness

Skills
- Creativity and Imagination

Materials
- Two or more familiar storybooks

How to Play
1. Have your child select a few of his favorite storybooks and hop into bed.
2. Let him decide which characters and setting he wants to use for his new story.
3. Have him pick out other details from each storybook.
4. Have him combine the elements from each story to make a completely new, wacky story.

Next Time
- Have your child select a favorite character. Suggest another character or setting and see what your child does with it.
- Have your child make up songs to accompany his stories.

Ages: 3 to 6 years

Night Owls

Has your child ever wondered what happens after she goes to sleep? Here's a chance for her to find out!

Values
- Emotional Expression

Skills
- Creativity and Imagination

Materials
- Nothing

How to Play
1. Have your child hop into bed.
2. Have her imagine what other people might be doing while she's asleep, such as working, playing, walking, traveling, watching TV, and so on.
3. Encourage her to be as creative as possible when describing what happens.

Next Time
- Have your child imagine what happens to the objects in her room after she goes to sleep. For example, does her stuffed animal come alive? What does it do? What about the toys, furniture, clothes, and so on?

Pick a Photo

When your child looks at a photo from the family album, does he remember the story behind the photo? I'll bet he'll have fun creating a whole new story!

Values
- Self-Awareness

Skills
- Creativity and Imagination

Materials
- Photos from the family album

How to Play
1. Have your child choose a photo and hop into bed.
2. Instead of talking about what really happened in the photo, have him make up a silly story that fits it.
3. See how wild he can make the story before you both collapse into giggles.

Next Time
- Choose four photos from different time periods. Line up the photos in any order and have your child tell a story based on them.

Ages: 6 to 10 years

Sensory Guess

Just before your child drifts off to sleep, help her get in touch with her senses and let them take her to slumberland.

Values
- Self-Awareness

Skills
- Creativity and Imagination
- Perception

Materials
- Three objects that can be identified by touch, smell, and hearing, such as a fuzzy teddy bear, a scented soap or candle, and a ticking clock

How to Play
1. Have your child hop into bed and close her eyes.
2. First let her touch one of the objects, such as the bear.
3. Then let her smell the second object, such as the soap.
4. Finally let her listen to the third object, such as the clock.
5. Have her keep her eyes closed and think about what the three objects are.
6. Challenge her to tell you what the three objects would make if they were combined. For example, the bear/soap/clock might be "a smelly bear clock."
7. Tell your child to go to sleep and dream about her new invention.

Next Time
- Have your child close her eyes and touch five objects, then see if she can identify them all.

Ages: 4 to 8 years

Stargazer

Your child doesn't have to go outside to see the stars. She can look for them on the ceiling!

Values

- Environmental Awareness

Skills

- Perception

Materials

- Flashlight
- Paper cup
- Skewer
- Tape

How to Play

1. Gather the flashlight, paper cup, and skewer.
2. Poke some holes in the bottom of the paper cup.
3. Put the paper cup over the lighted end of the flashlight and tape it on.
4. Have your child hop into bed.
5. Turn off the lights so the room is dark.
6. Have your child shine the flashlight on the ceiling and watch the stars come out.

Next Time

- Cut out designs in the paper cup before attaching it to the flashlight. Shine it on the ceiling and watch the image appear!

Ages: 3 to 6 years

Storybook Hunt

Have your child go on a treasure hunt right inside his storybook. See what he can find!

Values
- Curiosity

Skills
- Language and Vocabulary

Materials
- Storybook (age appropriate)

How to Play
1. Have your child choose a storybook and hop into bed.
2. Choose a picture or word anywhere in the book, and tell him to look for it while you're reading the book.

Next Time
- Give your child the book and have him find five to ten objects on his own.

Tell the Future

Can your child tell the future? Sometimes, if he looks hard enough, he can see what's going to happen!

Values
- Positive Attitude

Skills
- Critical Thinking

Materials
- Calendar
- Marker

How to Play
1. Get a calendar and marker and have your child hop into bed.
2. Have your child talk about his day while you write down the highlights.
3. Have him talk about what might happen tomorrow.
4. Have him decide what he's looking forward to tomorrow, and write these events on the calendar.
5. Check the calendar the next day to see if his predictions came true.

Next Time
- Have your child start a diary to write in every day.

What Happens Next?

Can your child guess what's going to happen next? Read a story and see if she's right!

Values
- Curiosity

Skills
- Creativity and Imagination

Materials
- New storybook (or one your child hasn't read)

How to Play
1. Have your child choose a new storybook and hop into bed.
2. Read the first page and have her guess what's going to happen next.
3. Do this on each page as you read the book.

Next Time
- Have your child make up her own story. Help her by asking, "What's going to happen next?"

Ages: 6 to 10 years

What's Wrong with This Room?

Something strange has happened in your child's room. Can he tell what it is?

Values
- Teamwork

Skills
- Perception

Materials
- Object in your child's bedroom, such as a stuffed animal, clock, picture, knickknack, or book

How to Play
1. Before your child goes to bed, sneak into his room and find an object you can move to another place.
2. Move the object so it's still visible from the bed but blends into the room. For example, you might switch a picture with a clock, move a stuffed animal to a new spot in the room, rearrange a couple of knickknacks, or turn your child's favorite book upside down.
3. Have your child get into bed, then look around the room and see if he can spot what's out of place.

Next Time
- Let your child move something and see if you can guess what it is.

Chapter Four

Car Time!

Ages: 4 to 12 years

Anywhere Bingo

Take along your own bingo game to play while you're in the car. Your child will have the whole world to play with!

Values
- Environmental Awareness

Skills
- Classification

Materials
- Pencil or pen
- Paper
- Clipboard, book, or other firm surface

How to Play
1. Draw a grid with five rows and five columns on the paper.
2. In each square, write the name of an item you're likely to see during your drive, such as *oak tree, blue bird, yellow house, man with a hat, gray cat, fire truck, gas station, crosswalk, bridge*, and so on.
3. Together, watch for the items during your trip and have your child check off the ones you spot.
4. You win the game when you've found five objects in one row, column, or diagonal.

Next Time
- Instead of trying to check off objects in a row, column, or diagonal, try to spot all the items on the card.

Ages: 6 to 12 years

Find a Letter

If your child knows his alphabet, he'll be great at this game. Keep your eyes peeled!

Values

- Setting Goals

Skills

- Language and Vocabulary

Materials

- Nothing

How to Play

1. Have your child choose a letter, then you choose a different one.
2. When you say, "Go," have your child begin looking for objects that begin with his letter. For example, if his letter is *p*, he should look for objects such as pavement, pet, peach tree, pizza place, pothole, poster, and so on.
3. Have him write down the names of the objects, or you can keep track for him by counting as he identifies objects. When his time is up, it's your turn.
4. See how many objects you can find in the time allowed.

Next Time

- Choose the same letter as your child and begin looking for objects that begin with that letter. The first one to name an object gets a point.

Ages: 6 to 10 years

From Here to There

Can your child find the shortest route from your starting point to your destination?

Values
- Environmental Awareness

Skills
- Map Reading

Materials
- Laminated map of the area
- Wipe-off marker

How to Play
1. Get a laminated map of the area in which you'll be traveling.
2. Mark the starting point and destination.
3. Give the map and wipe-off marker to your child.
4. Ask your child to highlight the shortest route to the destination using the marker.
5. Follow his route to see how long it takes and how well it works.

Next Time
- See if your child can find an interesting route instead of a short one.

Ages: 8 to 12 years

Historical Treasure Hunt

Can your child find the interesting or historically significant sites along your route? Have him pretend it's a treasure hunt!

Values
- Environmental Awareness

Skills
- Perception

Materials
- Detailed map of the area in which you'll be traveling
- Paper and pencil
- Marker

How to Play
1. Find a map that includes information about interesting sites along your route.
2. Write down the names of these sites on a separate sheet of paper.
3. Mark the starting point and destination of your trip on your map.
4. Describe one of the sites to your child and see if he can guess what it is. For example, for the California Redwood Forest you might say, "There are a lot of very old plants." Then ask him to find it on the map.
5. See how many points of interest your child can identify and find on the map.

Next Time
- Tell your child which direction to go and how far to travel. Have him follow this course on a map. See where he ends up!

Ages: 8 to 12 years

Make It Better!

Everything can stand a little improvement. This time, have your child focus on improving the world around her.

Values
- Environmental Awareness

Skills
- Critical Thinking

Materials
- Interesting things to look at

How to Play
1. While riding in the car, look out the window and try to spot something interesting, such as a construction site, run-down store, park, shopping center, and so on.
2. When you find something, point it out to your child.
3. Ask her to name one way she might improve it. For example, if it's a construction site, she might say, "Plant a flower garden around it." If it's a run-down store, she might say, "Give it a paint job."
4. Take turns pointing out things and finding ways to improve them.

Next Time
- Find more than one way to improve something. Take turns until you run out of ideas.
- After your child suggests improvements, encourage her to think of compliments, too.

Ages: 4 to 6 years

Name That Sign

This game will encourage your child to recognize street signs.

Values
- Environmental Awareness

Skills
- Classification

Materials
- Nothing

How to Play
1. While riding in a car together, you and your child each try to be the first to spot every street sign and call out what it says, for example: "stop sign" or "railroad crossing."
2. If the sign indicates an action, that also must be called out, for example: "Speed limit fifty-five miles per hour; slow down."
3. If there's a sign your child doesn't recognize, you call it out. Next time that sign appears, your child may recognize it.

Next Time
- Call out products advertised on bilboards, for example: "Big Mac" or "Whopper."

Ages: 4 to 8 years

Noisemakers

You hear lots of interesting noises while traveling in a car, but none as fun as the ones you make yourself!

Values
- Environmental Awareness

Skills
- Creativity and Imagination

Materials
- Nothing

How to Play
1. Roll up the windows so you can't hear the noises outside.
2. Make a funny or interesting noise that sounds like something outside, such as a car motor, train whistle, fire alarm, cat's meow, and so on.
3. Have your child repeat the noise, then add one of his own.
4. Take turns repeating the noises (all of them in order) and adding new ones until someone forgets one of the noises.

Next Time
- Try to correctly identify the noises the other person makes.

Ages: 5 to 10 years

Number Story

Use numbers to help create fun stories while driving.

Values
- Teamwork

Skills
- Math
- Problem Solving

Materials
- Nothing

How to Play
1. Think of a topic for your story, such as aliens from outer space, treasure hunting on a tropical island, exploring caves, and so on.
2. Begin the story by using the number 1. For example, you might say, "One day I went for a walk in the forest."
3. Have your child continue the story by including the number 2. For example, she might say, "The forest was dark, and I heard two strange sounds."
4. Continue taking turns telling the story and using numbers in ascending order until you reach 10.

Next Time
- Instead of using numbers in ascending order, use them in any order, but make sure you never use the same number twice.
- Try to begin and/or end each sentence with a number.

Point and Pretend

Does your child ever wonder what some of the things he sees out the window are used for? In this game, it's up to him!

Values

- Resourcefulness

Skills

- Critical Thinking

Materials

- Nothing

How to Play

1. Point to something interesting or unusual out the window, such as a silo, a rope swing, an antenna, a sculpture, a climbing structure, a bulldozer, or a flag.
2. Ask your child to imagine how the object might be used. Encourage him be as creative as possible.

Next Time

- Have your child give each object a name that matches the function he's described.

Ages: 7 to 12 years

Sign Story

Can your child make up a history for something along your route?

Values
- Resourcefulness

Skills
- Creativity and Imagination

Materials
- Nothing

How to Play
1. As you travel through new towns, watch for interesting names on the signs, such as Buzzard Hill Road; Jail Street; Truth or Consequences, New Mexico; and Weed, California.
2. Have your child tell a story about how each place got its name. For example, maybe Buzzard Hill Road used to have a lot of buzzards on the hill, and Jail Street may have once had a jail. Perhaps Truth or Consequences was a gambling town, and Weed was just a bunch of weeds at one time.
3. See who can come up with the most interesting story for each sign.

Next Time
- Instead of making up stories about names on signs, tell stories about things you see, such as a water tower, bridge, old barn, big rock, or odd landmark. Explain how each thing got there and what's it's used for.

Ages: 4 to 8 years

Super Powers

What would your child do if she had a special power? Have her imagine one and find out!

Values
- Self-Esteem/Self-Awareness

Skills
- Creativity and Imagination

Materials
- Nothing

How to Play
1. Have your child imagine she has a special power such as super strength, x-ray vision, the ability to fly, super smell, invisibility, and so on.
2. Ask her what she'd do with this super power. See how many things she can come up with.
3. Ask her how she might help others with the super power.

Next Time
- Have your child choose a new super power each time you take a drive.
- Have her choose her favorite super powers.

Ages: 4 to 8 years

Talk to the Animals

Has your child ever wondered if animals can talk? See if he can talk like the animals!

Values
- Respect for Nature

Skills
- Communication

Materials
- Animals

How to Play
1. While you're driving along the road, look around for an animal (cat, dog, horse, cow, bird, squirrel, chipmunk, and so on).
2. Have your child talk the way he thinks the animal would talk.
3. See how creative he can be with his voice and words.

Next Time
- Have a conversation with your child using animal talk.
- Think of animals you're not likely to see along the road, such as a zebra, elephant, pig, hippo, and so on. Have your child choose one and then talk like the animal.

Ages: 6 to 12 years

What If?

We don't usually think of problems as fun, but this game invites your child to enjoy herself by imagining both problems and solutions!

Values
- Positive Attitude

Skills
- Problem Solving

Materials
- Nothing

How to Play
1. Think of a problem to solve, such as "What would you do if you ran out of money?" or "How would you take care of a giraffe in your yard?" or "How would you survive on a deserted island?"
2. Have your child come up with at least three solutions.
3. Take turns coming up with problems and solutions.

Next Time
- Each time your child solves a problem, add something to make it worse. Then have her solve it again.

Where Are We Now?

Can your child guess where he is when his eyes are closed?

Values
- Environmental Awareness

Skills
- Perception

Materials
- Nothing

How to Play
1. When you're ready to begin driving along a familiar route, have your child close his eyes or blindfold himself.
2. As you travel along, have him guess where he is. Let him roll down the window if he wants more information.
3. Occasionally take a different turn to see if you can fool him.
4. Ask him questions about the landscape as he's identifying your location.

Next Time
- Have your child tell you how to get home—with his eyes closed!

Ages: 7 to 12 years

Which Way?

Try this game whenever you have some spare time on your hands. You never know where you'll end up!

Values
- Environmental Awareness

Skills
- Memory

Materials
- Map of the area

How to Play
1. If you find yourselves with some free time in the car, let your child take over giving directions.
2. Have her decide where she wants you to turn, and follow her directions wherever they lead.
3. As you go, ask her where she thinks the road will lead.
4. Ask her why she chose a certain turn.
5. After you've driven around a bit, see if she can get you back to where you started.

Next Time
- Plan your trip ahead of time by using a map.

Chapter Five

Kitchen Time!

Ages: 6 to 10 years

Add a Task

Make your child's chores fun by seeing how many tasks he can keep track of.

Values
- Achievement/Success

Skills
- Following Directions

Materials
- Simple tasks to perform such as setting the table, picking up toys, brushing teeth, folding towels, feeding the cat, and so on

How to Play
1. Give your child directions for a simple task such as setting the table. Have him perform the task.
2. When the task is finished, give him directions for doing two tasks.
3. When he's completed both tasks, give him directions for three tasks, and so on.
4. See how many tasks he can remember and carry out.

Next Time
- Instead of tasks, give your child stunts to perform. Have him do one, then add a new one each time. For example, start by having him jump across the room. Then have him jump across the room and somersault back. Continue adding stunts and see how many he can keep track of.

Ages: 3 to 6 years

Beat It

Have your child create his own concoction while you're cooking up a meal.

Values
- Curiosity

Skills
- Cooking
- Measuring

Materials
- Plastic bowl
- Water
- Teaspoon
- Liquid dish soap
- Eggbeater
- Food coloring

How to Play
1. Fill a plastic bowl with warm water.
2. Add a teaspoon of dish soap.
3. Have your child beat the soapy water with an eggbeater.
4. Add a few drops of food coloring and have him beat some more.
5. See what happens!

Next Time
- Try different soaps such as Ivory Flakes, shampoo, and so on.
- Let your child beat an egg to help with the cooking.

Ages: 3 to 6 years

Bowl Toss

How's your child's aim? See if she can fill up all the bowls!

Values
- Perseverance

Skills
- Perception

Materials
- Variety of plastic or metal bowls in different sizes
- Beanbags, marshmallows, balls, or other soft objects to toss

How to Play
1. Set up the bowls on the kitchen floor.
2. Place the smaller bowls closer to your child and the larger bowls farther away.
3. Have your child toss various objects into the bowls. See how many she can make!

Next Time
- Assign a point value to each bowl and keep track of the points.
- Have your child try tossing while blindfolded.
- Set the bowls on top of boxes or other sturdy objects.

Dessert Decorating

Let your child decorate the dessert and make it a festive centerpiece for the table.

Values

- Teamwork

Skills

- Creativity and Imagination

Materials

- Cake, pie, cookies, or other dessert
- Tubes of frosting
- Candy decorations, sprinkles, or other toppings

How to Play

1. Prepare a dessert your child can decorate.
2. Set the dessert on the table along with the frosting tubes and toppings.
3. Let her decorate the dessert any way she wants. Give her ideas, if necessary.
4. Showcase it for all to see.

Next Time

- Let your child help you make the dessert, too.

Ages: 8 to 12 years

Draw a Recipe

Whenever you cook or bake, your child can create an illustrated recipe for the dish you're making. Before long you'll have a unique and beautiful family cookbook!

Values
- Teamwork

Skills
- Communication
- Cooking

Materials
- Paper
- Markers
- Three-ring binder

How to Play
1. Get out paper and markers.
2. As you cook or bake, tell your child what you're doing. Explain what ingredients and equipment you're using, the quantities and measurements, and the steps in the process.
3. Have her write the recipe as you explain it.
4. Have her draw pictures that correspond with the recipe.
5. Save your child's handiwork in a three-ring binder. Add to the binder whenever you try a different recipe.

Next Time
- Help your child use the recipe she wrote and illustrated to make the dish again.

Ages: 4 to 8 years

Grocery Grouping

While you're unpacking the groceries, let your child sort them into different groups and figure out how they're similar and different.

Values
- Self-Reliance

Skills
- Classification

Materials
- Variety of food and non-food items

How to Play
1. Remove groceries from bags.
2. Let your child sort the items any way he wants, such as by color.
3. Suggest different ways to sort the items, such as food versus non-food, cooked versus uncooked, canned versus boxed, natural versus processed, or healthy versus unhealthy.
4. As he sorts the items, talk about how they're similar and different and why they're sorted a particular way.
5. Ask your child to put the items away when you're finished.

Next Time
- Have your child classify non-food kitchen items such as cooking utensils, appliances, bowls, silverware, and so on.
- Have your child sort and classify bedroom items.

Ages: 5 to 10 years

Make a Mix

Have your child make his own trail mix for snack time, movie time, or lunch time.

Values
- Self-Reliance

Skills
- Measuring

Materials
- Medium-size bowl and spoon
- Variety of trail mix ingredients such as granola, raisins, nuts, chocolate chips, chopped dried fruit, pretzel bits, sunflower seeds, and so on
- Measuring cups
- Plastic baggies

How to Play
1. Set out a bowl and spoon.
2. Let your child choose from a variety of trail mix ingredients.
3. Talk about his selections and what wouldn't be good in the mix.
4. Have him measure reasonable quantities of each ingredient, add them to the bowl, and stir with the spoon.
5. Have him scoop individual servings into plastic baggies.
6. Encourage him to share his trail mix with family and friends, and have him save some for lunch or snack time.

Next Time
- Have him try a different combination of items.

Ages: 7 to 12 years

Pancake Creatures

Pancakes aren't just for eating. They're also for creating crazy creatures!

Values

- Resourcefulness

Skills

- Cooking
- Creativity and Imagination

Materials

- Pancake batter, frying pan, vegetable oil spray or butter, and spatula
- Spoon, baster, or funnel
- Syrup, jam, and/or powdered sugar

How to Play

1. Make pancake batter and heat the frying pan. Coat the pan with vegetable oil spray or butter before adding batter.
2. Warn your child about the hot pan.
3. Have her use a spoon, baster, or funnel to drizzle the batter into the pan and make shapes.
4. Have her carefully flip the pancake shapes over, finish cooking them until light brown, and remove them with a spatula.
5. Ask her to identify the pancake critters she's made.
6. Serve with syrup, jam, and/or powdered sugar.

Next Time

- Have her help you make the batter, too.
- Add food coloring to the batter.

Patterns

Can your child follow the pattern? After he's done, maybe he can eat it!

Values
- Achievement/Success

Skills
- Critical Thinking

Materials
- Several bowls
- Variety of small food items such as cereals, nuts, candies, beans, and so on

How to Play
1. Fill several bowls with small food items, one item per bowl.
2. Design a pattern using the items, and have your child examine it. You might lay down two Cheerios, two beans, two candies, two Cheerios, two beans, and so on. Make it challenging but not too difficult for your child to figure out.
3. Have him continue the pattern once he thinks he understands it.
4. Talk about how different patterns are made.

Next Time
- Make the pattern more difficult each time you play.

Ages: 3 to 8 years

Play Clay

Let your child have fun combining various ingredients in the kitchen. She'll learn lots of valuable information as she conducts her first experiments.

Values
- Resourcefulness

Skills
- Creativity and Imagination

Materials
- 4 cups flour, 1 cup salt, and 1 3/4 cups water
- Large bowl, cooking utensils, and waxed paper

How to Play
1. Have your child combine the ingredients in a large bowl and knead the dough until it's smooth.
2. Provide him with various cooking utensils such as a plastic knife, garlic press, rolling pin, cookie cutters, and so on.
3. Place the dough on waxed paper and let him explore it with the utensils.
4. When he's finished, place the dough back in the bowl and cover well. The dough will keep for several weeks, if covered.
5. If your child wants to preserve one of the objects he creates, set the object on a piece of foil and bake it at 250°F for an hour or two until firm.

Next Time
- Have your child experiment with other ingredients and create a new kind of dough.

Ages: 10 to 12 years

Price Is Right

Has your child seen the price of groceries today? Can she guess how much various foods cost?

Values
- Environmental Awareness

Skills
- Value of Money

Materials
- Variety of foods and their prices

How to Play
1. As you unload groceries in the kitchen after a trip to the supermarket, remove the price tags (if there are any) and place them under the items.
2. Have your child try to guess the price of each item.
3. Let her check the price of each item (by looking at the price tag or the store receipt) to see how well she guessed.
4. Have her put each item away before she tries to guess the next item.

Next Time
- Have your child guess the price of other items, such as utensils, toys, books, and so on.

Seed Mosaic

Instead of cooking with seeds and beans, have your child make a beautiful mosaic with them.

Values
- Emotional Expression

Skills
- Creativity and Imagination

Materials
- Seeds, beans, cereals, and other small food items
- Small bowls
- Stiff paper
- White glue

How to Play
1. Pour various food items into small bowls, one item per bowl.
2. Set out paper and glue.
3. Have your child make a design by gluing the items onto the paper.
4. Allow plenty of time for the glue to dry.

Next Time
- Let your child finger paint with pudding on a large sheet of paper or a smooth countertop.

Ages: 4 to 8 years

Smell and Tell

Can your child tell a food by its smell? Have him take a whiff!

Values
- Environmental Awareness

Skills
- Classification

Materials
- Variety of food items with distinctive odors, such as ketchup, vinegar, orange juice, onion, vanilla, and so on
- Bowls
- Dishtowels
- Blindfold (optional)

How to Play
1. Choose a variety of items for your child to smell. Keep them covered so he can't see them.
2. Have him smell each item, one at a time. Use a blindfold if necessary.
3. Ask him to identify the item. Provide clues if necessary.

Next Time
- Instead of identifying the item, have your child describe the smell. (He may end up with the same response for several items.)
- Give him two smells at the same time and see if he can identify both.

Ages: 4 to 8 years

Spoon Shuffle

Can your child make it from one side of the kitchen to the other without spilling the food?

Values
- Self-Confidence

Skills
- Coordination/Balance
- Fine Motor
- Gross Motor

Materials
- Large spoon
- Small food item to carry in the spoon, such as a walnut, marshmallow, grape, small cracker, and so on

How to Play
1. Give your child a large spoon.
2. Place a small food item in the spoon.
3. See if your child can move across the room holding the food item in the spoon without spilling it.
4. See if she can go faster each time.
5. Try a variety of foods to see what adjustments she makes to avoid spilling the food item.

Next Time
- Have her try it with her eyes closed.
- See how far she can go without spilling the food item.

Ages: 3 to 6 years

Tong Thumbs

Your child may be all thumbs in the kitchen, but what would happen if she were all tongs?

Values
- Perseverance

Skills
- Problem Solving

Materials
- Several bowls
- Variety of items to pick up, such as a hard cracker, marble, sponge, spoon, egg, and so on
- Kitchen tongs

How to Play
1. Set out several bowls on the floor or table.
2. Place the items to be picked up on the floor or table nearby.
3. Give your child tongs and have her try to pick up the items and place each in a different bowl.

Next Time
- Have your child carry the items a few feet to the bowls.
- Make the items more and more challenging (smaller, more slippery, awkward to hold, and so on).
- Have your child try the game while blindfolded.

Ages: 4 to 10 years

Toothpick Play

It's amazing what your child can create with a few simple items and some toothpicks.

Values
- Resourcefulness

Skills
- Creativity and Imagination
- Fine Motor

Materials
- Toothpicks
- Playdough

How to Play
1. Take out a box of toothpicks.
2. Give your child some playdough, or have him make his own by combining 2 cups flour, 1/2 cup salt, and 3/4 cup water.
3. Let your child create something using the playdough and toothpicks.

Next Time
- Have your child use larger structural items such as skewers and Popsicle sticks to help him create bigger things.

Chapter Six

Mealtime!

Changeable

Are your children too busy eating to notice the changes in your family?

Values
- Importance of Family

Skills
- Perception
- Social Interaction

Materials
- Articles of clothing and other elements of appearance

How to Play
1. Before your family comes to the table, have everyone change one thing about his or her appearance. For example, you might wear different glasses, put your watch on the other arm, untie your shoes, wear someone else's T-shirt, and so on.
2. After you sit down, take turns guessing what's different about each person at the table.
3. Write down your answers individually (or remember them), so everyone has a chance to guess.
4. When everyone's ready, take turns sharing your answers.

Next Time
- Change some things about the dinner table, such as glasses, napkins, salt and pepper shakers, tablecloth, and so on. See how many changes your children can identify.

Ages: 8 to 12 years

Debate

It's easy for your child to argue his side of the story, but can he argue the other side?

Values
- Morals and Beliefs

Skills
- Critical Thinking

Materials
- Interesting topics for discussion

How to Play
1. Gather at the table and pick an interesting (and perhaps controversial) topic to discuss, such as "Would you steal money to help a sick person?" or "Should we use animals for scientific research?"
2. Ask your child which side he agrees with. Then ask him to defend the other side. When he's finished, argue his side.
3. Take turns stating your arguments, and see how many statements you can make to defend your positions.
4. Discuss the importance of seeing both sides of an argument.
5. When the argument is over, call it a draw.

Next Time
- Take turns defending the opposite sides of other issues.

Ages: 3 to 8 years

Face Food

Have your family members ever noticed their food staring back at them from their plates?

Values
- Emotional Expression

Skills
- Creativity and Imagination

Materials
- Variety of foods
- Garnishes to enhance your creations, such as sprouts, cherry tomatoes, parsley, shredded lettuce, carrot rounds, raisins, and so on

How to Play
1. Gather at the table.
2. As your family members fill their plates with food, have them arrange it to look like funny faces. For example, they might use mashed potatoes for cheeks, salad for hair, meat for a smile, a roll for a nose, and cherry tomatoes for eyes.
3. When all the faces are finished, show them to each other! Then gobble up your food before it gets cold!

Next Time
- Instead of making faces, make animals, buildings, landscapes, or whatever comes to mind. Have each family member guess what the others have made.

Family Awards

Give awards to one another during the evening meal. Be creative!

Values
- Importance of Family

Skills
- Critical Thinking

Materials Needed
- Paper and markers

How to Play
1. Give everyone a marker and enough sheets of paper for each family member.
2. Before dinner begins, have each person write an award for each family member. For example, you might choose "funniest," "loudest burper," "biggest eater," and so on.
3. During dinner, take turns sharing your awards with the rest of the family.

Next Time
- Have the winners each give a short acceptance speech.
- Create awards for other relatives and friends.

Ages: 5 to 12 years

Family Resemblance

How is your child similar to other family members? How is she different? Even if yours is an adoptive or blended family, you've got plenty in common!

Values
- Importance of Family

Skills
- Social Interaction

Materials
- Nothing

How to Play
1. Start the game by choosing one person at the table.
2. The rest of the family members take turns stating one way they are similar to the chosen person—in appearance, mannerisms, abilities, preferences, and so on.
3. Let each family member have a turn as the chosen person.

Next Time
- Compare and contrast yourselves with a movie star, sports figure, or other famous person.
- Compare and contrast yourselves with your pet!

Ages: 7 to 12 years

Fancy Folding

Brighten up your table with some fancy napkin folding.

Values
- Resourcefulness

Skills
- Creativity and Imagination

Materials
- Paper napkins

How to Play
1. Give everyone a couple of paper napkins.
2. Have everyone put a napkin in his or her lap to use for dinner.
3. Challenge each person to transform the second napkin by opening it up, then folding and/or tearing it to create an animal, person, flower, snowflake, or abstract shape.
4. When everyone is finished, take turns holding up your creations and trying to guess what they are.

Next Time
- Get an origami book from the library and try a new simple origami project at each meal.

Ages: 6 to 10 years

Funny Foods

Your child will have lots of fun eating foods that have funny names!

Values
- Positive Attitude

Skills
- Creativity and Imagination

Materials
- Meals or snacks

How to Play
1. Gather the family at the table.
2. Set the food on the table, and ask family members to give each food a funny name such as "whipped clouds" for mashed potatoes, "pig jerky" for bacon, "tri-corner toasties" for pizza, and so on.
3. Take turns sharing the funny names and explaining how each person thought them up.

Next Time
- Have everyone think of interesting inventions to use at the table. Have them imagine funny names for the inventions, such as "pea splitter" to cut peas in half, "salt spreader" to spread the salt evenly over the food, and so on.

Ages: 8 to 12 years

Guess the Food

Can your child identify a dish by hearing the list of ingredients?

Values
- Curiosity

Skills
- Classification

Materials
- Packaged foods that contain several ingredients, such as pizza sauce, cereal, pork and beans, soup, and so on
- Paper bags

How to Play
1. Before calling your family to the table, select a package of food for each player.
2. Place each food in a paper bag so no one can see what it is.
3. Gather at the table and give one bag to each player.
4. Have each player read the last ingredient listed on his or her food container, without letting other players see it.
5. Have other players try to guess the food.
6. Continue reading the ingredients from last to first until someone guesses the food.

Next Time
- Try different foods each time you play.
- Play with non-food items such as toothpaste, shampoo, shaving cream, and so on.

Ages: 7 to 12 years

How Well Do You Know Me?

Do your family members really know each other as well as they think?

Values
- Importance of Family

Skills
- Social Interaction

Materials
- Paper and pencils

How to Play
1. Gather at the table and choose a category such as desserts, drinks, stores, magazines, rock bands, and so on.
2. Announce one of the categories and have family members write down their favorites in that category.
3. Then have each person write down what he or she thinks is each family member's favorite in that category.
4. Take turns reading the answers. Award a point for each guess a player gets right.
5. Add up the points to find out who knows the other family members best.

Next Time
- Choose a different category each time you play.

Ages: 8 to 12 years

Match Game

Can your family members match each other's answers?

Values

- Respect for Others

Skills

- Social Interaction

Materials

- Paper and pencils

How to Play

1. Gather at the table and choose a category such as vegetables, song titles, movie actors, candy bars, and so on.
2. Announce the category to the family and have each person write down what he or she thinks most of the players will choose. For example, if the category is vegetables, someone might write down *potato* thinking that most of the players will do the same.
3. Keep the papers hidden until everyone has written down answers.
4. Turn the papers over and see how many players have the same answers.
5. Each player who matches the most popular answer for the category gets a point.
6. Choose another category and play again.
7. The player with the most points at the end wins.

Next Time

- Play the opposite way, in which everyone tries not to match the others' answers.

Mealtime Designs

Design a fancy tablecloth to make mealtime more festive!

Values
- Emotional Expression

Skills
- Creativity and Imagination

Materials
- Plain paper tablecloth or old, clean sheet
- Variety of markers

How to Play
1. Spread a tablecloth or sheet over the table.
2. Set the table with plates, silverware, glasses, and so on.
3. Set out colorful markers in the middle of the table.
4. Have family members draw designs at their places while they eat.
5. When the meal is over, remove the plates and enjoy what you've created together!

Next Time
- Choose a theme for your tablecloth, such as "Our Neighborhood," "Our Family Portraits," or "Favorite Foods." Work on it together.

Ages: 7 to 12 years

Secret Dessert

It's just as fun to guess what dessert might be as it is to eat it. (Well, almost.)

Values
- Teamwork

Skills
- Critical Thinking

Materials
- Dessert

How to Play
1. Make a special dessert for the family.
2. After dinner, have all the family members take turns asking yes-or-no questions to help them guess what's for dessert. Tell them they can't just call out the names of desserts. They must ask questions like "Is the dessert red?" "Is it sweet?" "Will it melt?" "Is it chewy?" "Is it made with flour?"
3. When someone thinks he knows what the dessert is, he may take a guess when it's his turn to ask a question. If he's right, he gets the first piece of dessert. If he's wrong, he's out of the game, and the rest of the players continue until someone guesses correctly.

Next Time
- Have your child help you make the dessert and lead the game.
- Have the family guess what's for dinner tomorrow night.

Switch Plates

Something magical happens when you sit in someone else's place at the dinner table.

Values
- Importance of Family

Skills
- Social Interaction

Materials
- None

How to Play
1. As your family gathers at the table, have everyone sit at someone else's place.
2. Have each person pretend to be the person who normally sits at that place. Without ridiculing, he or she should act like the person, talk like the person, and try to be the person for the entire meal.
3. After the laughter subsides, talk about how accurate each person's impersonation was.

Next Time
- Have each family member impersonate a non-family member such as a friend or movie star. Have other family members try to guess who's being impersonated.

Ages: 4 to 10 years

Taste Test

Does your child really taste his food? Have him find out how good his taste buds really are!

Values
- Environmental Awareness

Skills
- Classification

Materials
- Variety of tasty foods

How to Play
1. Choose several foods that are interesting to taste, such as ketchup, mustard, tomato sauce, different kinds of crackers, different cheeses, different kinds of ice cream, and so on.
2. Have your child close his eyes and give him one of the foods to taste.
3. Have him describe the taste.
4. Have him guess what the food is.

Next Time
- Make up new names for familiar foods based on what they taste like.

Ages: 5 to 12 years

Thank Goodness

Dinner time is the perfect time to express why you're thankful for each other.

Values
- Emotional Expression
- Importance of Family

Skills
- Social Interaction

Materials
- Paper and pencils

How to Play
1. Write down the names of each person at the table, one name per sheet.
2. Gather at the table and place the papers in the middle.
3. Let everyone choose a name.
4. Go around the table and have all the family members tell why they're thankful for the people they chose.
5. When everyone has had a turn, put the papers back in the middle and have everyone choose again.

Next Time
- Have all the family members talk about other things they're thankful for, such as the Earth, their friends, their home, and so on.

Ages: 7 to 12 years

Winker

Can your child eat and talk and wink all at the same time?

Values
- Achievement/Success

Skills
- Social Interaction

Materials
- Deck of cards

How to Play
1. Pull out enough cards (one red, the rest black) so there's one for each player.
2. Gather everyone at the table.
3. Shuffle the cards and pass them out facedown.
4. The person with the red card is the Winker. She must try to "catch" each person at the table by winking at them without being seen by someone else.
5. If the Winker winks at everyone without getting caught, she wins the game.
6. If the Winker gets caught by someone before she catches everyone, she loses.
7. Mix up the cards and play again.

Next Time
- Instead of winking, make a funny face.

Chapter Seven

Outdoor Time!

Adopt Your Neighborhood

Businesses are adopting highways to keep them clean. You and your child can do something similar in your neighborhood.

Values
- Environmental Awareness
- Helping Others

Skills
- Recycling

Materials
- Garbage bags, gloves, and pointed sticks for spearing trash
- Paper and pencil

How to Play
1. Have your child look around the neighborhood and see if there's any litter to be picked up. If he looks hard enough, he'll probably see things that need to be thrown away.
2. Get a garbage bag and work together to collect as much trash as you can.
3. When you get home, write down how much trash you found.
4. Do the same thing the following week. See if there is less trash each time you collect it.

Next Time
- Expand your trash collection to include your local school, park, church, synagogue, and so on.

Ages: 5 to 12 years

Balance Beam

Outside is the perfect place for your child to practice her Olympic skills.

Values
- Perseverance
- Self-Confidence

Skills
- Coordination/Balance
- Gross Motor

Materials
- Objects to use for skill building, such as a rope, hose, bench, tire, and so on

How to Play
1. Choose an object to represent an Olympic event, such as a curb or fallen tree for the balance beam.
2. Have your child try walking along the balance beam without falling off.
3. Have her try walking the balance beam in a variety of ways such as sideways, backward, eyes closed, and so on.

Next Time
- Have your child practice other Olympic skills such as using a bench as a pommel horse, jumping over water from a hose, hopping inside a tire, and so on.

Ages: 6 to 10 years

Balloon Blast

Keep a few balloons in your pocket or purse and you'll always have something fun to do.

Values

- Resourcefulness

Skills

- Gross Motor

Materials

- Balloon

How to Play

1. Blow up a balloon and tie the end for your child.
2. See how long she can keep the balloon up in the air by batting it with her hands.
3. Count the number of times she's able to bat the balloon.

Next Time

- Blow up and tie a balloon for yourself, too, and race your child from one end of the outdoor area to the other, keeping your balloons up in the air. If a balloon touches the ground, its owner must go back to the starting point and begin again.
- Try keeping a balloon in the air with your head only—no hands!
- Blow up a balloon, but don't tie the end. Make squeaking noises by stretching the end and letting air seep out slowly.
- Blow up a balloon, but don't tie the end. Let go of it and watch it fly around crazily! See if your child can catch it before it lands on the ground.

Ages: 7 to 10 years

Bird Calls

Is your child fascinated by birds? He can spend some time with his feathered friends when he does this chirpy activity.

Values
- Respect for Nature

Skills
- Memory
- Perception

Materials
- Area with birds

How to Play
1. While you're outside, listen for the sound of birds.
2. Challenge your child to imitate the calls of different birds.
3. Pretend to have a conversation in "bird talk."

Next Time
- Make up some new bird calls.
- Tape-record some real bird calls and some of your own calls, then compare and contrast the two.

Crayon Rubbings

Have your child reproduce objects from nature. Put her artwork on the wall for everyone to admire.

Values
- Environmental Awareness

Skills
- Classification

Materials
- Flat objects from nature
- Sheets of paper
- Crayons

How to Play
1. Have your child collect flat objects from nature, such as leaves, flowers, dead insects, and so on.
2. Place each object on a flat surface, and place a sheet of paper on top.
3. Let your child color gently over the paper until an image of the object appears.
4. Repeat for the other objects and see how they turn out.

Next Time
- Don't let your child see the object as you place the paper on it. Let her guess what it is as it appears in her drawing.

Ages: 8 to 12 years

Flight School

Send a paper aircraft soaring in the great outdoors.

Values
- Curiosity

Skills
- Fine Motor
- Math

Materials
- 8½" x 11" paper

How to Play
1. Fold a sheet of paper into an airplane: (a) Fold the paper in half so the fold is parallel to the long sides. Lay the folded paper on a table so the fold is nearest you. (b) Grasp the right edge (one layer only) and fold it toward you so it meets the first fold. (c) Grasp the fold you just made and fold it toward you so it meets the first fold. (d) Repeat step c. (e) Flip the paper over and lay it so the first fold is nearest you. (f) Grasp the left edge (one layer only) and fold it toward you so it meets the first fold. (g) Repeat steps c and d.
2. Have your child throw the airplane.
3. Mark the landing spot and see if your child can throw the airplane farther each time.

Next Time
- Teach your child how to fold his own paper airplane.
- Try to design your own paper airplane together.
- Decorate your airplane with stickers and markers.

Ages: 5 to 10 years

Is It Nature or Not?

Does money grow on trees? Does milk come from a carton or a cow? How well does your child know what comes from nature?

Values
- Environmental Awareness

Skills
- Classification
- Critical Thinking

Materials
- Variety of objects

How to Play
1. Take a walk outside together.
2. Select objects as you walk along, such as wooden fences, candy wrappers, cement, matchsticks, and so on.
3. Talk about whether they're natural or made by people.
4. Talk about where things come from, and see if your child can trace a certain object (such as mulch) back to nature.

Next Time
- Look at items in nature and sort them into categories such as animal, plant, dead, alive, edible, nonedible, poisonous, nonpoisonous, and so on. Bring books along to help you classify the objects.

Ages: 6 to 12 years

Lawmaker

If your child doesn't like what's happening to the environment, have him think of ways to change it.

Values
- Respect for Nature
- Setting Goals

Skills
- Critical Thinking

Materials
- Problems in the environment

How to Play
1. As you walk along or drive through your neighborhood, have your child search the environment for problems such as too many freeways, no landscaping, not enough trees, pollution, crowded conditions, and so on.
2. Have your child write a letter to a government agency about his environmental concerns.

Next Time
- Ask your child to make up new laws that would help these environmental problems. Talk about what would happen if the laws weren't enacted.
- See if your child can find other problems he'd like to fix at home, in school, and in other places.

Ages: 3 to 6 years

Match a Leaf

Can your child tell one type of leaf from another? Leaves are like snowflakes—no two are alike. But lots are similar!

Values
- Environmental Awareness

Skills
- Classification

Materials
- Several types of leaves

How to Play
1. Go outside and have your child collect several kinds of leaves, two of each kind.
2. Mix up the leaves and set them on the ground.
3. See if your child can match each leaf with its pair.
4. Talk about how the leaves are similar and different.

Next Time
- Make a collage with the leaves.
- Get a book on trees and learn the names of trees and where different leaves come from.

Ages: 6 to 10 years

Nature Bugs

You can invent your own insects with objects you find in nature.

Values
- Resourcefulness

Skills
- Creativity and Imagination

Materials
- Small natural objects, such as leaves, twigs, shells, flowers, pods, seeds, and so on

How to Play
1. As you enjoy the outdoors, collect a variety of small natural objects together.
2. When it's time to rest, choose a smooth area and set out all the objects you've collected.
3. Have your child arrange some of the objects into the shape of a new insect. For example, she might use a leaf for a body, twigs for legs, and seeds for eyes.
4. Have your child give her new insect an interesting name, such as "podpillar," "daddy twiglegs," "eight-legged spiderfly," or "leafadopterus."

Next Time
- Bring paper and glue so your child can turn her new bug into a permanent picture for her room.
- Bring a book about insects and see how many different kinds your child can spot.

Ages: 8 to 12 years

Nature Hunt

Go on a scavenger hunt in the great outdoors and see how many things your child can find.

Values
- Environmental Awareness

Skills
- Classification

Materials
- Pencil, pen, or marker
- Paper bag

How to Play
1. Think up ten things that can be found outdoors, such as a feather, a pine cone, a dead insect, a two-color leaf, a snail shell, a piece of bark, a pod, a round rock, a three-inch twig, and an acorn.
2. Write the list on a paper bag.
3. Head outside and see how many items your child can find on the list.
4. See how long it takes him to find all the items.

Next Time
- Write the same list on two bags. Race to find the items on the list and see who can find them all first.
- Have a scavenger hunt for different kinds of litter instead of nature items, and do the earth a favor while you play.

Ages: 6 to 12 years

Neighborhood Hunt

How well does your child know his neighborhood?

Values
- Environmental Awareness

Skills
- Map Reading

Materials
- Paper and pencil

How to Play
1. Walk around your neighborhood.
2. Look for new, unusual, or interesting things, such as an anthill, bird's nest, tree stump, and so on.
3. When you get home, quiz your child about where you saw each interesting object.

Next Time
- Draw a map to help you find the interesting objects again on your next walk.

Ages: 5 to 10 years

Shadow Shapes

Capture the Shadow Shapes before they disappear!

Values
- Teamwork

Skills
- Creativity and Imagination

Materials
- Sunshine
- Colored chalk
- Pavement

How to Play
1. Choose a sunny day and head outside with chalk.
2. Stand on the pavement and cast an interesting shadow. For example, shape your hands in the form of an animal, figure, design, and so on.
3. Have your child draw the shadow shape on the pavement with colored chalk.
4. See how it turns out. Discuss other ways to interpret the shadow.
5. Take turns shaping, drawing, and interpreting.

Next Time
- Place your body in an interesting position. For example, you could pretend to be reaching for something, running somewhere, or acting out something. Have your child draw the shadow from your body shape. Have her add details to create a superhero, monster, costumed character, or anything she wants. Take turns creating interesting shapes and drawings.

Ages: 4 to 8 years

Shape Shifting

Have your child imagine what things would be if they weren't what they are!

Values
- Environmental Awareness

Skills
- Creativity and Imagination

Materials Needed
- Nothing

How to Play
1. As you walk together outside, look for an object with an interesting shape, such as a tree, rock, bush, flower, fence, light post, and so on.
2. Have your child study the object for a few minutes, and ask her to imagine what it looks like. For example, a gnarled old tree could look like an old man, a space alien, or a monster. A jagged rock could look like a spaceship, dinosaur, or castle.
3. Find other objects and have your child imagine what they could be.

Next Time
- Use metaphors to describe what you see. For example, a tree might be a "tall tin soldier" or a "giant fluffy feather."

Ages: 4 to 10 years

Touch and Tell

Let your child's fingers figure out what's in the bag.

Values
- Environmental Awareness

Skills
- Critical Thinking
- Fine Motor
- Perception

Materials
- Objects in nature such as leaves, twigs, rocks, flowers, and dead bugs
- Paper bag

How to Play
1. Choose some objects from nature and put them in a paper bag without letting your child see them.
2. Have your child close her eyes, and give her one of the objects.
3. Have her touch the object and describe its characteristics.
4. Have her guess what it is.

Next Time
- Add some objects that are not from nature and see if your child can describe them and identify them.

Chapter Eight

Play Time!

Ages: 6 to 10 years

Animal Alphabet

Your child can turn anything into an animal, even a letter of the alphabet!

Values
- Resourcefulness

Skills
- Creativity and Imagination

Materials
- Paper and pencil or marker

How to Play
1. Get out lots of paper and a pencil or marker.
2. Draw a large letter of the alphabet on the middle of the paper.
3. Ask your child to turn the letter into an interesting animal.
4. Try to guess what the animal is when she's finished.
5. If it doesn't look like a familiar animal, give it a funny name.

Next Time
- Have your child turn numbers into monsters, squiggly lines into landscapes, her name into an insect, and so on.

Ages: 8 to 12 years

Card Construction

Take turns adding cards to your construction and see what you end up with!

Values
- Teamwork

Skills
- Creativity and Imagination
- Fine Motor

Materials
- Scissors
- Old deck of playing cards or set of index cards

How to Play
1. With the scissors, cut two quarter-inch slits into each long side of each card. Cut each slit about a half-inch from the corner of the card. Leave the short sides of the card intact.
2. Build a card construction with your child by taking turns adding one card at a time. Link the cards together at the slits.
3. Keep adding cards until you run out of them or you're satisfied with your creation.
4. When the card construction is finished, have your child explain what it is and give it an interesting name.

Next Time
- Take turns adding cards vertically until the construction collapses.

Ages: 6 to 10 years

Crazy Creatures

Have your child create puppets from everyday items!

Values
- Emotional Expression

Skills
- Creativity and Imagination
- Language and Vocabulary

Materials
- Objects that can be converted into puppets, such as socks, small towels, teddy bears, balls, blocks, clothespins, and so on
- Markers, wiggly eyes, or round, colorful stickers

How to Play
1. Have your child look around for two objects that can be transformed into puppets. Encourage her to be creative! Other examples include paper bags, small boxes, washcloths, plastic cups, and so on.
2. Draw eyes, a nose, and a mouth on the puppets with markers. You could also glue on wiggly eyes or stick on dots.
3. Let your child imagine a conversation between the two puppets.

Next Time
- Have your child create a skit for the puppets and put on a show.

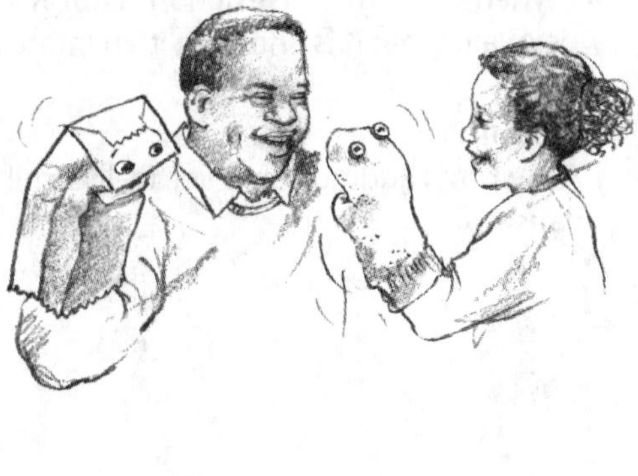

Ages: 3 to 6 years

Dinosaurus Rex

Have your child make up her own dinosaurs and imagine what they'd do if they lived today!

Values
- Resourcefulness

Skills
- Creativity and Imagination

Materials Needed
- Paper and markers

How to Play
1. Have your child imagine a new type of dinosaur.
2. Have her draw it on paper and give it a special trait such as breathing fire, having two heads, being invisible, and so on.
3. Have her give it a special name to go with the special trait. For example, a fire-breathing dinosaur might be called Flamosaurus. An invisible dinosaur might be called Invisisaurus Rex.

Next Time
- Have your child draw a new animal that's a combination of two different animals. For example, she might draw a dog-cat, chicken-elephant, or turtle-kangaroo! Have her give the new animal a special name such as Puppypuss, Chickaphant, or Turtleroo.

Ages: 6 to 12 years

Dress-Up Designers

Your child will have a ball changing his identity every time he changes his appearance.

Values
- Resourcefulness

Skills
- Creativity and Imagination

Materials
- Old clothing and accessories from your closet or a thrift shop

How to Play
1. Collect some old clothes and accessories. You might include skirts and dresses, baggy pants or shorts, shirts, vests, gloves, hats, shoes, costume jewelry, ties, and scarfs.
2. Put the clothes in a box and let your child choose items to create different costumes.
3. Have your child put on a fashion show or act out a story using the different costumes.

Next Time
- Collect many different kinds of hats and other head coverings, such as a firefighter's hat, cowboy hat, scarf, sailor's cap, top hat, stocking cap, crown, bridal veil, baseball cap, party hat, and hardhat. Have a "hat day" and wear different hats throughout the day, acting like different characters according to the hats you're wearing.

Ages: 7 to 12 years

Focus

Can your child draw what she sees through a tube? Have fun guessing what it is!

Values
- Environmental Awareness

Skills
- Fine Motor
- Perception

Materials
- Paper towel (or toilet paper) tube
- Paper and pencil

How to Play
1. Have your child look at something through a paper towel (or toilet paper) tube.
2. Have her draw only what she sees through the tube.
3. After the picture is finished, have her show it to you.
4. Try to guess what it is.

Next Time
- Instead of letting your child choose what to look at, have her close both eyes as you position the tube. Then have her open one eye and look through the tube. Ask her to draw the object she sees. When she's finished, have her look at the picture and guess what she drew.

Ages: 8 to 12 years

Footsy Art

Can your child be an artist by using only his foot?

Values
- Resourcefulness

Skills
- Creativity and Imagination

Materials
- Paper and pencil
- Tape

How to Play
1. Place a sheet of paper on the floor and tape it down so it doesn't move.
2. Have your child take off his shoe, and place a pencil between his toes.
3. Have him draw a picture of something.
4. When he's finished, see if you can guess what it is!

Next Time
- Have your child try toe painting (using fingerpaints with his toes), sponge painting with his feet, making footprint animals, and other fun tricks with his feet.

Ages: 6 to 10 years

How Old Are You?

You're only as young (or old) as you think.

Values
- Emotional Expression

Skills
- Social Interaction

Materials
- Deck of cards

How to Play
1. Mix up the facedown cards and have your child pick two from the pile.
2. Turn them faceup and read the age that's been created. For example, if you see a 2 and a 7, the age is 27. If you see an 8 and a 2, the age is 82. If one of the cards is a face card, select another card until you get a number card.
3. For the next few minutes, act and talk the age represented in the cards.

Next Time
- Gather some props to enhance the game.
- After you've determined the age, determine the gender by having your child select a card until she chooses a face card. The gender of the face card determines how you should act.

Ages: 6 to 10 years

Hypnotized

Has your child ever been hypnotized? Let him find out what's it like to be in a "trance."

Values
- Teamwork

Skills
- Creativity and Imagination
- Following Directions

Materials
- Object to use for hypnotizing, such as a dangling watch or moving wand

How to Play
1. Find an object to hypnotize your child with, and explain what you're going to do.
2. Wave the object in front of his eyes to put him in a "trance." He must act like a zombie, speak in a monotone, and try to keep his eyes straight ahead.
3. Think of things for him to do while in the "trance," such as set the table, take out the garbage, brush his teeth, get your slippers, and so on.
4. He must do what you say, but don't make the task too complicated or unpleasant. Just have fun with it.

Next Time
- Let your child hypnotize you!

Ages: 3 to 8 years

Musical Art

Your child doesn't have to be musically inclined to enjoy musical art. Just have her draw her emotions as she listens to the music!

Values
- Emotional Expression

Skills
- Creativity and Imagination

Materials
- Variety of music
- Paper and colored markers

How to Play
1. Choose a variety of music.
2. Give your child some paper and colored markers.
3. Play the first selection and have her draw how the music makes her feel.
4. Change the music every few minutes. Give her a fresh sheet of paper each time, and have her draw to the new music.
5. When she's finished, look at her pictures and see if you can tell which pictures match the music you played.
6. Talk about how the music made her feel and why she drew differently to different kinds of music.

Next Time
- Instead of choosing music beforehand, turn on the radio and go up and down the dial. Have your child draw to whatever music comes on.
- Have your child keep the same sheet of paper but choose a different marker to draw with whenever the music changes.

No Peeking

How well can your child do a task without looking?

Values
- Resourcefulness

Skills
- Problem Solving

Materials
- Items used for an activity, such as building a Lego creation or dressing a doll

How to Play
1. Assemble the materials for a task or activity.
2. Have your child close her eyes and tell her to do the task or activity.
3. When she's finished, have her open her eyes and see how she did. Have fun laughing together at the silly things that may have happened—perhaps your child put the doll's pants on its arms or built a Lego car with five wheels!

Next Time
- Have your child try to do the same activity with one hand or no hands.

Ages: 4 to 8 years

Personal Placemats

Have your child use his artistic ability to liven up the dinner table!

Values
- Emotional Expression
- Importance of Family

Skills
- Fine Motor

Materials
- Construction paper
- Craft materials such as markers, crayons, or fingerpaints
- Clear Contact paper

How to Play
1. Set out some construction paper and craft materials.
2. Have your child think of a theme for decorating the placemats, such as vacation plans, holidays, healthy foods, animals, and so on.
3. Have him decorate a placemat for each family member.
4. Preserve the finished placemats by covering them with clear Contact paper.

Next Time
- Have your child design puzzles, dot-to-dot pictures, or other games on the placemats. Your family will have fun playing while they eat.

Ages: 7 to 12 years

Rule Reversal

Change the rules of familiar games for some new and challenging fun.

Values

- Resourcefulness

Skills

- Problem Solving

Materials

- Items needed for a game, such as tick-tack-toe, hopscotch, or marbles

How to Play

1. Assemble the materials needed for the game you want to play.
2. Play the game with the rules or the object of the game reversed. For example, if you're playing tick-tack-toe, try to *avoid* getting three Xs or three Os in a row. If you're playing hopscotch, work your way from the *end* of the hopscotch court to the beginning. If you're playing marbles, try to shoot a marble into a circle full of marbles *without* knocking any of the marbles out of the circle.

Next Time

- Think of other activities you can do in reverse. For example, read a story from end to beginning or eat a meal from dessert to main dish to salad.

Ages: 3 to 8 years

Tea Party

Have an old-fashioned tea party and spend some time sipping and chatting with your child.

Values
- Importance of Family

Skills
- Language and Vocabulary
- Social Interaction

Materials
- Fruity teas (decaffeinated) or milk and honey
- Cookies
- Fancy tablecloth and small table
- Tea set

How to Play
1. Help your child make some fruity tea, or warmed milk with honey.
2. Make some cookies together or buy them from the store.
3. Set the table with a nice tablecloth and tea set.
4. Put on fancy clothes, if you like.
5. Sit at the table, pour the tea, and serve the cookies.
6. Have a nice chat about interesting topics while enjoying your tea and cookies.

Next Time
- Have a special lunch, snack, or dessert.

Ages: 6 to 10 years

Toe Art

Has your child ever tried to draw a picture with his toes instead of his fingers?

Values
- Resourcefulness

Skills
- Fine Motor
- Gross Motor

Materials
- Crayon or marker
- Paper

How to Play
1. Remove your shoes and socks.
2. Insert a crayon or marker between your child's big toe and the next toe. Do the same for yourself.
3. Challenge your child to draw something in the room with his toes. Do the same yourself.
4. See if you can identify the things depicted in each other's drawings.

Next Time
- Draw pictures with your hands—but blindfolded.

Ages: 8 to 12 years

Truth or Dare

Your child will enjoy the challenge of telling the truth or doing a dare! Which will it be?

Values

- Morals and Beliefs

Skills

- Problem Solving

Materials

- Scissors
- Paper and pencil

How to Play

1. Cut sheets of paper into small squares.
2. On half of the squares, write questions such as "Have you ever told a lie?" "Have you done anything wrong this week?" "Which movie star do you have a crush on?" and so on.
3. On the rest of the squares, write dares to perform, such as "Jump backward across the room," "Do a somersault," "Sing 'The Star-Spangled Banner,'" and so on.
4. Take turns choosing a truth or dare.

Next Time

- Instead of choosing a truth or dare, flip a coin to determine whether you must answer a question or do a dare.

Ages: 7 to 10 years

Yarn Shapes

Your child can draw with a pencil, but can she make a picture with a piece of yarn?

Values
- Resourcefulness

Skills
- Creativity and Imagination

Materials
- Yarn

How to Play
1. Have your child shape an animal or object with yarn on the table or floor.
2. When she's finished, try to guess what the shape is.
3. Take turns making shapes and figuring out what they are.

Next Time
- Make shapes using other materials such as beads, mosaic pieces, scraps of fabric, feathers, pipe cleaners, and so on.

Chapter Nine

Quiet Time

Ages: 8 to 12 years

Body Codes

Occasionally your child may want to "say" something to you without using words. Here's a fun way for him to share his thoughts and feelings.

Values
- Emotional Expression

Skills
- Communication

Materials
- Paper and pencil

How to Play

1. Have your child write down some thoughts or feelings he might like to share with you during quiet time or when he's around other people and doesn't want them to know what he's saying. For example, he might write "I'm bored," "I'm hungry," or "Let's go."
2. Have him think of gestures or "body codes" that signify his thoughts or feelings. For example, if he wants to say "I'm bored," he might tap his fingers on the back of his hand. If he wants to say "I'm hungry," he might draw a circle on his stomach. If he wants to say "Let's go," he might flick his finger twice.
3. Review the gestures until you know them by heart.

Next Time
- Have your child use facial expressions to communicate messages (winking, grimacing, lip smacking, eyebrow lifting, and so on).

Ages: 8 to 12 years

Can You Read Me?

Can your child understand what you're saying when you only mouth the words?

Values
- Teamwork

Skills
- Communication

Materials
- Your mouths

How to Play
1. Have your child choose a topic to discuss, such as her plans for the day, something she likes to do, her favorite food, her favorite TV show, and so on.
2. Have a conversation with each other using only your lips—not your voices—and see if you can understand each other.
3. If you have trouble understanding each other, mouth the words slowly but don't exaggerate your lips. Repeat if you have to.

Next Time
- To help your child communicate without speaking, have her act out the information while she mouths the words.

Ages: 6 to 10 years

Change, Please

Instead of counting the minutes, have your child count the money.

Values
- Responsibility

Skills
- Math
- Value of Money

Materials
- Variety of coins
- Egg cartons
- Coin wrappers

How to Play
1. Take out some loose change from your pocket, purse, or change bucket.
2. Have your child use egg cartons to sort the change into pennies, nickels, dimes, quarters, and half-dollars.
3. Have him count the coins and place the correct amount in the wrappers.
4. Take the coins to the bank and exchange them for dollars, or put them in a savings account.

Next Time
- Place a dollar on the table along with your loose change. See if your child can find the exact amount of change to match the dollar.

Ages: 7 to 12 years

Fantasy Day

Your child can have any kind of day he wants if he uses his imagination.

Values
- Positive Attitude

Skills
- Creativity and Imagination

Materials
- Paper and pencil

How to Play
1. Have your child imagine his perfect day.
2. Have him write down the times, locations, and other details of his fantasy day.
3. Have him save this sheet of paper for years to come, to find out how many parts of his fantasy day came true.

Next Time
- Have your child write down certain things he wants to do each day for an entire week. Help him accomplish his goals.

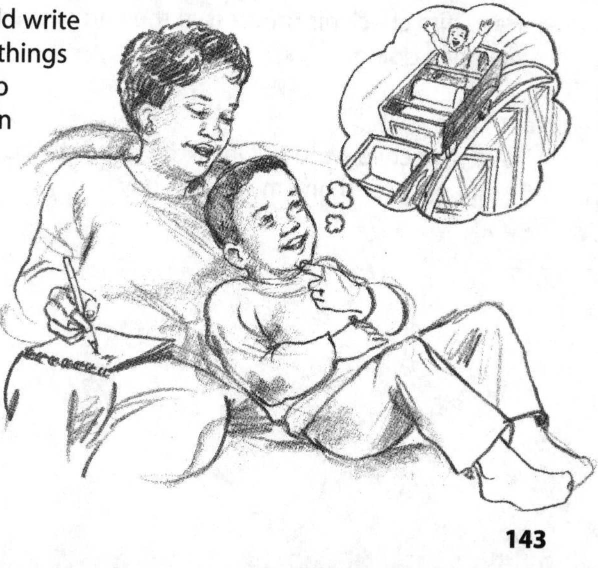

Ages: 8 to 12 years

Habitudes

What would your child change about his "habitudes?"

Values
- Self-Awareness

Skills
- Critical Thinking

Materials
- Paper and pencil

How to Play
1. Have your child make a list of all his good habits (doing his homework right after school, cleaning up his messes, saying his prayers, and so on).
2. Have him write down his bad habits (forgetting to brush his teeth, burping and not saying "Excuse me," not picking up his clothes, and so on).
3. Have him think about one of his bad habits and work on changing it into a good habit over the next week or so.
4. Have him check his progress at the end of the week to see how he's doing.

Next Time
- Have your child write down all the good things he did that day. See if he can add one more each day.

Ages: 8 to 11 years

Hand Talk

Your child's hands will come in handy in this nonspeaking game. She doesn't need to know sign language to communicate with her hands!

Values
- Emotional Expression
- Resourcefulness

Skills
- Communication

Materials
- Hands

How to Play
1. Have your child think of something to say, such as what happened that day, what her plans are tomorrow, or news about herself.
2. Have her try to express her words using only her hands.
3. Guess what she's trying to communicate.
4. Take a turn talking with your hands while she guesses.
5. See if you can have a conversation using only your hands.

Next Time
- Look through a magazine for interesting pictures, and pick one without letting the other person see it. Try to communicate what the picture means using only your hands. Have the other person guess.
- Act out scenes from movies you've seen together or books you've read together. Guess the titles.

Ages: 8 to 12 years

Photographic Memory

Does your child have a photographic memory? Find out how much he can remember.

Values
- Achievement/Success

Skills
- Memory

Materials
- Magazine picture

How to Play
1. Find an interesting magazine picture.
2. Have your child study it for one minute and try to remember as many details as he can.
3. Remove the picture.
4. Ask him questions about the picture.

Next Time
- Instead of asking your child questions about the picture, have him write down as many details as he can remember.

Ages: 6 to 12 years

Stamp It

How many things can you use to make a stamp picture?

Values
- Resourcefulness

Skills
- Creativity and Imagination

Materials
- Paper
- Ink pad or poster paint in a saucer
- Objects that can be used for stamping, such as thread spools, film canisters, sponges, foam pieces, toy cars, pencil erasers, plastic animals, fruit and vegetable pieces, leaves, flowers, and so on

How to Play
1. Give your child some paper and an ink pad or poster paint in a saucer.
2. Collect objects that can be used for stamping.
3. Have your child press an object onto the ink pad or into the paint and then press it onto the paper.
4. See what kinds of designs your child can make with each object.

Next Time
- Have your child use her fingertips as stamps.
- Have your child embellish her stamped designs with markers.
- Have your child show her stamped designs to others and challenge them to guess the object that made each imprint.

Ages: 8 to 12 years

Stick 'Em Up

Surprise one another with special sticky notes.

Values
- Importance of Family

Skills
- Communication

Materials
- Sticky notes and pencil

How to Play
1. Entertain each other by writing creative messages on sticky notes. You might write "Happy Birthday," "Have fun at your first day of school," "Enjoy your day off," and so on.
2. Place them all over the other person's room for a surprise.

Next Time
- Place the sticky notes in unexpected places such as the bathroom, closet, car, and so on.
- Write a story that continues from note to note.
- Create a treasure hunt using sticky notes, leading the other person all over your home.
- Draw cartoons instead of writing notes.

Ages: 6 to 10 years

String Along

Have your child follow the string and see where it leads!

Values
- Perseverance

Skills
- Gross Motor
- Perception

Materials
- Skein of string or yarn

How to Play
1. Find a skein of string or yarn long enough to stretch throughout your home or yard.
2. Tie one end of the yarn to a reward, such as a book to read, a game to play, or a snack.
3. Unravel the yarn and wind it around different items in your home or yard.
4. When you're finished, give the free end to your child.
5. Have her follow the yarn to the reward.
6. Take turns creating a yarn maze and following it throughout your home or yard.

Next Time
- Make a path of seeds or stones to indicate which way to go.

Ages: 8 to 12 years

Tabloid News

Your child can create her own outrageous headlines with a plain old newspaper. You'll both get a laugh out of what's (not really) happening.

Values
- Communication

Skills
- Language and Vocabulary

Materials
- Newspaper
- Scissors
- Large sheet of paper
- Glue or tape

How to Play

1. Together, scan the newspaper for interesting headlines, such as "Dog Bites Man," "Baby Born in Car," or "American Wins Top Award." Cut out the headlines and set them aside.
2. Scan the newspaper for interesting photos, such as a picture of a cute puppy, a small man, a baby, a car, and a pie-eating contest. Cut out the photos and set them aside.
3. Have your child arrange the headlines and photos on the large sheet of paper in a funny way, then glue or tape them down. For example, under the headline "Dog Bites Man," she might put the picture of the puppy with the small man in its mouth. Under the headline "Baby Born in Car," she might put the picture of the car with the baby in the driver's seat. Under the headline "American Wins Top Award," she might put the picture of the pie-eating contest.

Next Time
- Write a funny story to go with each headline and photo.

Ages: 8 to 12 years

Thanks a Lot

Writing thank-you notes can be fun for the writer and reader!

Values
- Emotional Expression

Skills
- Language and Vocabulary

Materials
- Note cards or paper
- Lemon juice
- Toothpicks or very fine paintbrush

How to Play
1. Have your child think of someone who deserves a thank-you note.
2. Have him write the note using a toothpick or very fine paintbrush dipped in lemon juice.
3. Send the note along with instructions to hold the note near an incandescent light bulb or iron it with a hot iron to make the writing appear.

Next Time
- Help your child make his own note paper or stationery using stamps and an ink pad.
- Write thank-you notes with different colored pens, sparkly pens, glitter pens, and so on.

Ages: 8 to 12 years

The Riddler

Can your child stump you? Can you stump your child?

Values
- Resourcefulness
- Sense of Humor
- Teamwork

Skills
- Critical Thinking
- Language and Vocabulary

Materials
- Book of riddles

How to Play
1. Find a book of riddles at the library or bookstore, or make up your own.
2. Take turns asking each other riddles and guessing the answers.
3. Give each other hints if necessary.

Next Time
- Have your child make up some riddles for you to answer.

Ages: 8 to 12 years

True or False?

Can your child tell what's true and what's not?

Values
- Honesty

Skills
- Critical Thinking

Materials
- Paper and pencil

How to Play
1. Have your child write down some questions for you, such as "What happened at work today?" "What do you want for your birthday?" "What's your favorite food?" and so on.
2. Have him ask one of the questions.
3. Provide three answers (two true, the other false). For example, if he asks, "What happened at work today?" you might answer, "I ate lunch. I filed a report. I talked on the phone." One of these answers must be false.
4. Have him try to pick out the false answer. If he gets it on the first try, he earns a point.
5. Take turns asking questions and keeping score.
6. When you've asked all your questions, add up the points.

Next Time
- Instead of giving three choices, ask each other true-or-false questions.

Ages: 8 to 12 years

Wacky Words

Can your child tell the meaning of a wacky word if you use it in a sentence?

Values
- Sense of Humor

Skills
- Creativity and Imagination
- Language and Vocabulary

Materials
- Paper and pencil

How to Play
1. Invent some wacky words such as "squiggum," "misslewhip," "flubdubit," and so on. Write them down on a sheet of paper.
2. Use one of the wacky words in a sentence.
3. Have your child try to guess the meaning of the word in the context of the sentence. Come up with other sentences if she can't figure out the meaning.
4. Take turns making up words, using them in sentences, and having the other person guess their meanings.

Next Time
- Have fun creating wacky names for objects around the home.

Ages: 4 to 8 years

What's the Connection?

Can your child figure out the connection among three objects?

Values
- Perseverance

Skills
- Classification
- Critical Thinking

Materials
- Paper and pencil

How to Play
1. Draw or write down three things that are connected somehow, such as pepperoni, cheese, and tomato (pizza); a hat, umbrella, and jacket (rain gear); words, pictures, and cover (book); and so on.
2. Have your child try to figure out the connection.
3. Give him hints if he needs help.
4. Take turns choosing the three words.

Next Time
- Play a game by choosing two objects and finding three ways they're connected. For example, if you choose a dog and a shoe, you might say, "They're both black, they're both soft, and they're both squeaky."

Chapter Ten

Shopping Time!

Ages: 7 to 11 years

Act It Out

Can your child "talk" with gestures instead of her mouth?

Values
- Emotional Expression

Skills
- Communication

Materials
- Nothing

How to Play
1. While you're out shopping, ask your child to see how long she can go without talking.
2. Have her use her body to mime what she wants to communicate to you.
3. When she's done, check to see if you understood her.
4. Try miming back to her. Go back and forth as long as you can.

Next Time
- Set a time limit and see if you can go the whole time without talking.

Ages: 7 to 12 years

Alien Explanation

Can your child explain our world to an alien visitor?

Values
- Environmental Awareness

Skills
- Communication

Materials
- Whatever products are available at the store(s) you visit

How to Play
1. Pretend you're an alien visiting planet Earth for the first time.
2. Have your earthling child explain what things are and how they work.
3. Ask questions (misunderstand at times) and make comparisons to objects on your alien planet.
4. Take turns being the alien and the earthling.

Next Time
- Ask your child what it's like on his planet and see what creative descriptions he can come up with.

Ages: 6 to 10 years

Alphabet Hunt

Can your child find all the letters of the alphabet before it's time to leave the store?

Values
- Perseverance

Skills
- Language and Vocabulary

Materials
- Signs and packaged products in the store

How to Play
1. Challenge your child to find all twenty-six letters of the alphabet in the store.
2. To play, he must first find a word that starts with the letter *a* on a package or a sign. Next he must find a word that starts with the letter *b*, and so on. For example, if you're at the supermarket, he might find the word *applesauce* on a jar of applesauce, then the word *bananas* on a sign in the produce department, and so on.

Next Time
- Instead of hunting for words, have your child look for numbers. See how many consecutive numbers he can find, starting with 1, then 2, then 3, and so on.

Ages: 8 to 12 years

Check the Change

Your child can help you make sure your transactions are always correct!

Values
- Value of Money

Skills
- Math

Materials
- Cash register receipt
- Pocket calculator (optional)

How to Play

1. When you get a receipt for a purchase, give it to your child and have her check the charge for each item (if there aren't too many items) and add all the charges to make sure the total is correct.
2. Next, tell her how much money you paid and how much change you got back. Have her subtract the latter from the former and find out whether the difference is the same as the total charge.

Next Time

- If you're buying lots of items (at the supermarket, for example), have your child spot-check the charges for several items rather than all of them.

Ages: 8 to 12 years

Comparison Shopper

Teach your child how to spot a bargain.

Values
- Resourcefulness

Skills
- Math
- Value of Money

Materials
- Nothing

How to Play
1. Choose a category in which there are a number of competitive products selling in the same quantity, such as a quart of milk, a pound of butter, and so on.
2. Have your child find the cheapest product in the category.
3. Have her figure out how much money she saved you.
4. Offer thanks for a job well done.

Next Time
- Choose a product category in which the cost is based on a certain price per unit of measurement. For example, certain cheeses are sold on a price-per-ounce basis. Have your child find the product that costs the least per unit.

Ages: 4 to 8 years

Find the Food

Make grocery shopping more fun by having your child find the items.

Values
- Teamwork

Skills
- Memory

Materials Needed
- Nothing

How to Play
1. As you go down each aisle of the grocery store, choose something for your child to find. (For safety's sake, be sure to keep an eye on her and stay nearby.) For example, if you're in the produce aisle, have your child try to find a kiwi fruit or navel orange or bean sprouts.
2. Every time you turn down a new aisle, give her another assignment.
3. Keep track of how many items she finds during the trip.

Next Time
- Have your child find a specific brand of food.
- Have her try to find all the ingredients for the evening meal.

Ages: 8 to 12 years

Gift Basket

While you're out shopping for yourselves, pick up a few things for those in need.

Values
- Helping Others

Skills
- Value of Money

Materials
- Paper and pencil
- Small amount of money/allowance

How to Play
1. When you enter a store, note whether it has a bin to collect donations for the needy. (Many grocery stores collect for food shelves, and during the winter holidays toy collection is common.)
2. While you're out shopping, have your child choose a few small items for donation. Discuss how practical the items are, how important they might be to a child or family, and so on.
3. Have your child purchase the items separately and deposit them in the bin on her way out of the store.

Next Time
- Have your child think of other ways she can help people who are less fortunate than she is.

Ages: 6 to 10 years

Guess the Grocery Bill

Enjoy your time in the checkout line by having your child guess what the total bill will be.

Values
- Resourcefulness

Skills
- Math
- Memory

Materials
- Cart full of groceries

How to Play
1. Fill your grocery cart and head for the checkout line.
2. Have your child examine the contents of your cart.
3. Ask him to guess what the total bill will be.
4. Give him a reward for getting close to the right answer (within ten dollars).
5. If his answer is very close (within five dollars), give him an extra special reward.

Next Time
- Make it a multiple-choice question. For example, if the bill is $98.03, give him that answer plus $84.55, $120.32, and $138.47. See if he can guess the right amount.
- Have your child guess the cost of an individual item.

Ages: 6 to 10 years

How Much for One Dollar?

How well does your child know the value of a dollar?

Values
- Resourcefulness

Skills
- Value of Money

Materials
- Dollar bill or a dollar in change
- Paper and pencil

How to Play
1. Take out a dollar bill or the equivalent in change.
2. Ask your child to guess what she can buy with a dollar. Have her make a list.
3. Give her the money and take her to a grocery/candy/dime store to see how much she can buy for a dollar.
4. Discuss what she can buy, what she might have to put back, and the difference between one price and another.
5. Ask her what she might do to earn more money to buy something more expensive.

Next Time
- Give your child chores to perform so she can earn more money for something she wants.
- Have your child set a goal of saving money.

Ages: 7 to 10 years

Magnetic Attraction

When your child has a magnet, she always has something to do!

Values
- Environmental Awareness

Skills
- Classification

Materials
- Small magnet
- Items in a store

How to Play
1. Have your child bring along a small magnet when you go shopping.
2. On the way to the store, have her guess what objects she'll find that will be magnetic.
3. If she has trouble thinking of things, offer her a choice between two objects and have her guess which one will be magnetic (for example, a pencil versus a metal pen, a plastic rack versus a metal rack, and so on).
4. Have her use the magnet to check the items when she gets to the store.
5. Have her find as many magnetic items as she can.

Next Time
- When you get home, have your child guess what household items are magnetic.
- Think of other places where your child can have fun with her magnet.

Ages: 7 to 12 years

Memory Test

While you're out shopping, test your memory skills and see how well you remember the details.

Values
- Teamwork

Skills
- Memory

Materials
- Nothing

How to Play
1. While you're out shopping, choose something interesting and have your child look at it for a few moments. You might choose a person, a product, a mannequin, a display, a sign, or anything else that offers some detail.
2. After your child has studied the selection, have him close his eyes or turn away.
3. Ask him some questions about the selection to test his memory. For example, if you've chosen a mannequin, you might ask the following questions: "What color is her hair?" "What does she have in her hair?" "Is she wearing glasses?" "What's on her arm?" "Is she wearing pants or a dress?" "Is she taller than me?" "What kind of shoes is she wearing?" and so on.
4. Let your child look at the selection to see how many details he got right.

Next Time
- Reverse roles and have you child choose an item to test your memory.

Ages: 7 to 10 years

Opposite Hand

Have your child put his nondominant hand to the test while you're out and about.

Values
- Resourcefulness

Skills
- Fine Motor

Materials
- Nothing

How to Play
1. While you're out shopping, have your child do everything with his nondominant hand. For example, if he's right-handed, he must do everything with his left hand, such as open a door, pick up objects, eat a snack, and so on.
2. Talk with him about what it's like to use your nondominant hand for tasks.

Next Time
- Have your child do everything with both hands at the same time.

Ages: 7 to 12 years

What Can You Do with a...?

Have your child find a common object and imagine its many uses.

Values
- Resourcefulness

Skills
- Creativity and Imagination

Materials
- Common object such as a sheet of paper, small box, piece of string, stick, candy wrapper, paper clip, and so on
- Paper and pencil

How to Play
1. Have your child find a common object while you're out shopping.
2. Have her think of all the ways she might use the object.
3. Give her paper and a pencil and have her write down the possible uses (or help her do it). For example, if she finds a sheet of paper, she might imagine folding it into an airplane, writing on it, tearing it up into confetti, wadding it into a ball, rolling it into a tube, cutting it into different shapes, and so on.

Next Time
- Have your child see how many objects she can "change" into something else.

Ages: 7 to 12 years

When I Grow Up

While you're at the store, think about what it would be like to work there.

Values

- Respect for Others

Skills

- Creativity and Imagination
- Critical Thinking

Materials

- Nothing

How to Play

1. The next time you're at a store, look around at the various people who work there, such as salespeople, cashiers, baggers, stockers, managers, custodians, security officers, information clerks, and so on.
2. Ask your child what he thinks it would be like to have the job of one of the workers he sees. For example, if he sees a supermarket cashier, ask your child what responsibilities that job might include, such as checking prices, scanning products, filling bags, taking money, making change, answering questions about food, and so on.
3. Discuss the pros and cons of each job. For example, a supermarket cashier might have to stand for a long time, but might also get to talk to lots of interesting people and get a discount on groceries.

Next Time

- Encourage your child to ask employees questions about their jobs. Ask your child if he would like to have a particular job.

Chapter Eleven

Sick Time

A Is for....

Your child needs only her eyes, mouth, and brain for this sick-in-bed game.

Values
- Perseverance

Skills
- Language and Vocabulary

Materials
- Nothing

How to Play

1. Look around your child's bedroom and find something that begins with the letter *a*. For example, you might see an apple, ant, airplane (toy), armchair, and so on.
2. Have your child find something that begins with the letter *b*, such as bed, blanket, ball, bear (teddy), and so on.
3. Take turns finding objects in alphabetical order.
4. Set a time limit (one minute), if you like.
5. Award a point for every correct answer.
6. The player with the most points when you reach the end of the alphabet wins the game.

Next Time

- Go through the alphabet several times. Quit when you get tired, then count up the points to see who won.
- Make up a story as you go along. For example, you might say, "One day an *ant* went to a picnic." Your child might say, "He crawled under a *blanket* and went to sleep."

Ages: 7 to 12 years

All About Me Poster

What would your child put on a poster that's all about him?

Values
- Emotional Expression
- Self-Esteem

Skills
- Classification

Materials
- Photo of your child
- Glue or tape
- Scissors, markers

How to Play
1. Glue or tape a photo of your child in the middle of the poster.
2. Have him use markers to add words and drawings that reflect his thoughts, ideas, and feelings.
3. Hang the poster on the wall.

Next Time
- Start a "Me Book" all about your child. Help him add pages every week.

Ages: 5 to 10 years

Bean Toss

Just because your child is sick doesn't mean she can't toss some beans!

Values
- Achievement/Success

Skills
- Fine Motor

Materials
- Cupcake pan
- Wipe-off markers
- Beans

How to Play
1. Set the cupcake pan a short distance from your child while she's lying in bed.
2. Use a wipe-off marker to number the cups inside the pan, giving each row a different value. For example, cups in the first row could be worth five points, the second row ten points, and so on.
3. Give your child a handful of beans and have her toss them into the cups.
4. Count how many points she scored.
5. Play again and see if she can beat her score.

Next Time
- Instead of a cupcake pan, use several measuring cups of different sizes.

Commercial Crazy

Are TV commercials creative or just plain crazy? Have your child decide.

Values
- Morals and Beliefs

Skills
- Critical Thinking

Materials
- TV commercials

How to Play
1. Watch kids' TV shows together while your child is lying in bed.
2. Listen to the commercials when they come on, then discuss them.
3. Decide what parts of the commercials are true and honest, and what parts are false or exaggerated.
4. Talk about how commercials try to convince you to buy something.
5. Talk about whether this is a good thing or not.
6. Ask your child what he would do if he were making a commercial or trying to sell a product.

Next Time
- Make it a memory game instead. Watch several commercials while watching a kids' TV show, then ask questions about them when the show is over. See how much your child can remember.

Ages: 5 to 10 years

Create a Holiday

Christmas, Hanukkah, Valentine's Day, Fourth of July.... You can never have enough holidays, right?

Values

- Resourcefulness

Skills

- Creativity and Imagination
- Planning/Scheduling

Materials

- Yearly calendar

How to Play

1. Look at the calendar with your child.
2. Have her think of new holidays to add to the calendar, such as Last Day of School, Clean Up the Neighborhood Day, Braces Off Day, First Sunny Day, Mother/Daughter Tea Day, and so on.
3. Have her talk about how she would celebrate the day. Discuss invitations, decorations, games, activities, refreshments, and favors.

Next Time

- Have your child fill in calendar squares with important family dates such as birthdays, anniversaries, trips, special events and honors, special beginnings or endings, and so on.

Ages: 4 to 8 years

Felt Fun

With just a few pieces of felt and a pair of scissors, your child can create an infinite variety of designs.

Values

- Resourcefulness

Skills

- Creativity and Imagination

Materials

- Scissors
- Felt in a variety of colors
- Baking sheet

How to Play

1. Help your child cut a piece of felt the size of the baking sheet and tape it to the back of the pan.
2. Help your child cut circles, squares, triangles, rectangles, ovals, half-circles, stars, and other shapes from the remaining felt.
3. Have your child stick the felt shapes to the felt-covered pan to create different designs and pictures, such as a house, a town, a face, an underwater scene, and so on. Encourage her to use her imagination.

Next Time

- Help your child cut pictures from magazines and glue them onto pieces of felt. Have her use the felt-backed pictures to tell a story.

Ages: 8 to 12 years

Finger Faces

If you've got a pair of hands handy, you've got some entertainment.

Values
- Emotional Expression
- Resourcefulness

Skills
- Creativity and Imagination

Materials
- Washable markers
- Fingertips
- Scissors, pieces of fabric, and tape

How to Play
1. Use the markers to draw funny faces on your child's fingertips.
2. Cut out pieces of fabric and tape them to her fingers to enhance the characters.
3. Have her act out a story with her fingertip friends.

Next Time
- Turn garden gloves into finger puppets by using markers to draw funny faces on the fingers.
- Have your child choose her favorite story and re-create the characters on her fingertips.

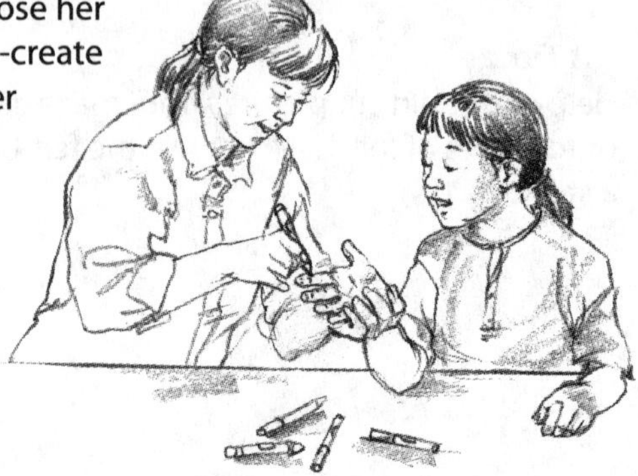

Fortunately/Unfortunately

How are things going? It all depends on your attitude.

Values
- Positive Attitude

Skills
- Critical Thinking

Materials
- Nothing

How to Play
1. Have your child think of a topic for a story, such as "a day at school," "getting sick," "finding a surprise," and so on.
2. Have her begin the story with a positive statement such as, "I was excited about my first day at school."
3. Have her continue the story by adding an unfortunate event such as, "On the way to school, I tripped on the sidewalk."
4. Have her alternate fortunate and unfortunate events while she tells the story.
5. Have her end the story on a positive note.

Next Time
- Make up a story together by having one person tell the fortunate events and the other person tell the unfortunate events.
- Have your child talk about a bad experience she had recently, and have her turn it into a happy story.

Magazine Scavenger Hunt

Your child can have a scavenger hunt without leaving his bed!

Values
- Setting Goals

Skills
- Classification

Materials
- Paper and pencil
- Magazines

How to Play
1. Make a list of items that would be fun for your child to find in magazines, such as medicine, food, clothing, jewelry, tools, cars, and so on.
2. Gather some magazines and make sure the items can be found in them.
3. Have your child open the first magazine and begin looking for the items on the list.
4. Have him check off an item when he finds it.
5. See how long it takes him to find all the items, or see how many he can find in a certain period of time.

Next Time
- Have your child make up a list of things for you to find.

Ages: 5 to 10 years

Make a Meal

Have your child create menus for meals in bed!

Values
- Resourcefulness

Skills
- Classification
- Planning/Scheduling

Materials
- Food magazines
- Scissors
- Construction paper
- Glue or tape

How to Play
1. Have your child choose a meal such as breakfast, lunch, or dinner.
2. Gather some food magazines and have her cut out pictures of food she would like to eat at the meal.
3. Have her fold a sheet of construction paper in half to make a menu.
4. Have her glue or tape the magazine pictures into the menu.
5. Have her choose another meal and make a menu for it.

Next Time
- Have your child use magazine pictures to design a wardrobe, toy store, bedroom, playroom, and so on.

Ages: 6 to 10 years

Mirror Image

Who does your child see looking back at her in the mirror?

Values
- Self-Esteem/Self-Awareness
- Sense of Humor

Skills
- Creativity and Imagination
- Fine Motor

Materials
- Portable mirror
- Wipe-off markers

How to Play
1. Give your child a portable mirror and some wipe-off markers.
2. Have her look in the mirror and use the markers to draw a funny face on her reflection. For example, she might draw a mustache, glasses, funny hair, freckles, big red lips, earrings, and so on.
3. Have her wipe off the funny face and make a new one.

Next Time
- Give your child a metal spoon and have her look at her reflection inside the spoon's bowl. Ask her: "Is it right side up or upside down?" "Is it bigger or smaller than your real face?" "Does your face look funny or normal?" Now have her look at her reflection on the other side of the spoon and ask her the same questions.

Ages: 8 to 12 years

Share a Sketch

Can two people draw a picture together? Grab some markers and find out!

Values
- Teamwork

Skills
- Social Interaction

Materials
- Paper and markers

How to Play
1. Have your child use a marker to draw a line on a sheet of paper.
2. Add to the line with your own marker.
3. Continue taking turns drawing until the picture is finished.
4. Talk about your ideas when you started and what happened as the picture developed.

Next Time
- Take turns drawing a person, animal, or object. See what you come up with.

Ages: 7 to 12 years

Shoelace Art

Have your child decorate her shoes while she's getting well.

Values
- Resourcefulness

Skills
- Creativity and Imagination
- Fine Motor

Materials
- Shoelaces and sneakers
- Permanent felt-tip markers

How to Play
1. While your child is lying in bed, have her spend time redecorating her sneakers and shoelaces.
2. Have her use markers to make dots, designs, stars, hearts, teddy bears, or anything she likes.
3. When she's finished, she'll have a colorful pair of shoes and shoelaces to match.

Next Time
- Have her decorate her pillowcase, T-shirt, nightgown, underwear, handkerchief, socks, and anything else you think is okay.

Ages: 8 to 12 years

Story Cards

With a set of picture cards, you can tell a different story every time you play.

Values
- Resourcefulness

Skills
- Creativity and Imagination

Materials
- Magazine pictures
- Index cards
- Scissors
- Glue

How to Play
1. Go through magazines together and cut out interesting pictures.
2. Glue the pictures onto index cards.
3. Mix up the cards and stack them facedown.
4. Have your child draw the top card and make up the beginning of a story using that picture.
5. You draw the next card and use that picture to add to the story.
6. Continue taking turns at drawing cards and adding to the story until someone draws the last card and brings the story to a close.

Next Time
- Write words on the index cards instead of using pictures.

Ages: 6 to 12 years

With and Without

If your child had to choose, what could she live without?

Values

- Emotional Expression
- Self-Reliance

Skills

- Critical Thinking

Materials

- Paper and pencil

How to Play

1. Have your child write down ten things she thinks she couldn't live without.
2. Have her write down ten things she wouldn't want to live without but could.
3. Have her write down ten things she could easily live without.
4. Talk about her choices.

Next Time

- Have your child think of ten things she'd like to take to different places such as a vacation destination, a desert island, outer space, the North Pole, school, and so on. Talk about her choices.

Ages: 7 to 10 years

World in a Box

Have your child create his own miniature world in a box!

Values
- Resourcefulness

Skills
- Creativity and Imagination

Materials
- Shoebox, construction paper
- Magazine pictures, greeting cards, inexpensive picture books
- Miniature people, animals, furniture, and so on
- Ribbon, scissors, glue, tape

How to Play
1. Find a shoebox and turn it on its side.
2. Have your child choose a theme for his world, such as Jungle World, Farm World, Space World, Underwater World, and so on.
3. Have him cut out pictures to illustrate his miniature world.
4. Fold the bottom edges of the pictures to help them stand up in the box. Glue or tape them securely.
5. Have him add miniature figures, landscaping, furniture, and so on.
6. Use ribbon to hang a sun, stars, or other items from the top of the box.
7. When you're finished, have him imagine a story to go with the scene.

Next Time
- Have your child create a miniature world in a fishbowl or terrarium.

Chapter Twelve

Waiting Time!

Ages: 7 to 12 years

Careers

Encourage your child to have fun imagining herself in various careers.

Values
- Setting Goals

Skills
- Critical Thinking

Materials
- Nothing

How to Play
1. Have your child think of what she might like to be when she grows up, such as a police officer, mail carrier, doctor, writer, and so on.
2. Have her act out the role.
3. See if you can guess what it is.
4. Take turns acting out careers for each other and guessing what they are.

Next Time
- Act out movie scenes, special events, holiday activities, the day's events, and so on.

Ages: 6 to 12 years

Color Meal

Can your child plan a whole meal in just one color?

Values
- Resourcefulness

Skills
- Classification

Materials
- Nothing

How to Play
1. Have your child choose a color.
2. See how many foods of that color you can come up with together. For example, if your child chose red, the menu might include tomatoes, strawberries, red meat, red potatoes, ketchup, and so on.
3. Take turns naming foods until someone gets stuck.
4. Have your child choose a new color and start over.

Next Time
- Name things of the chosen color in different categories, such as flowers, toys, clothing, animals, and so on.

Daffynitions

Have fun with your child by making up words and their definitions.

Values
- Resourcefulness

Skills
- Language and Vocabulary

Materials
- Nothing

How to Play
1. Have your child make up a funny word such as "sniggle-wiggle," "fangalino," "mushygush," and so on.
2. Ask her to think of a definition for the word.
3. Have her use the word in a sentence.
4. See how many times she can use the word the rest of the day.

Next Time
- Take turns making up words and definitions.
- Have your child think of real words, and ask her to define the words as best she can. Look up the definitions to see how close she was.

Ages: 3 to 8 years

Eyewitness

How many details can your child remember about something that happened?

Values
- Environmental Awareness

Skills
- Memory
- Perception

Materials
- Nothing

How to Play
1. While you're waiting in line, have your child watch for something to happen, such as a person buying something, a nurse calling a patient, and so on.
2. When something happens, identify it and ask your child if he noticed.
3. Ask him questions about what happened, such as, "What was the person wearing?" "What did she say?" "How tall was he?" "Which way did she go?" and so on.
4. See how many details your child can remember.
5. Take turns watching scenes and recounting the details.

Next Time
- Act out a scene and have your child tell you what happened in as much detail as possible.
- Take turns acting out scenes.

Goody Bag

Your child will always have something to do if you take along a goody bag full of surprises.

Values

- Resourcefulness

Skills

- Creativity and Imagination

Materials

- Bag
- Various goodies such as crayons, paper, Slinky, yo-yo, toy binoculars, deck of cards, dice, puppet, favorite book, and so on

How to Play

1. Select a special bag to hold the goodies.
2. While you're waiting in line, have your child feel the bag and guess what's inside.
3. Let her take something out and play with it any way she likes.
4. Each time you go somewhere, put something new in the goody bag and bring it along.

Next Time

- See if your child can think of ten ways to play with the goody toy.
- Have your child suggest what goodies to put in the bag.

Ages: 6 to 12 years

Guess Who

Can your child guess a famous or familiar person before he uses up twenty questions?

Values
- Teamwork

Skills
- Classification

Materials
- Nothing

How to Play
1. Think of a famous person, such as Britney Spears or Superman, or a familiar person, such as Grandmother or the mail carrier. The person may be real or fictional.
2. Have your child ask yes-or-no questions to help him guess the person you're thinking of. For example, he might ask, "Is the person male?" "Is the person under twenty-one years old?" "Is the person real?" "Is the person famous?"
3. When your child thinks he knows who the person is, he may ask, "Is it ______?"
4. Keep track of how many questions your child asks. If he asks twenty questions without guessing the person you're thinking of, announce the answer.

Next Time
- Have your child try to guess an object or a place instead of a person.
- If your child gets stuck, give him a clue. Each clue counts as one question.

Magazine Match

See who can find the most matches in a waiting-room magazine.

Values
- Setting Goals

Skills
- Classification

Materials
- Magazine

How to Play
1. Find a waiting-room magazine or bring your own magazine.
2. Have your child choose a category that can be found in the magazine, such as food, clothing, jewelry, medicine, cars, sweets, and so on.
3. Turn the pages and see how many objects in the category you can find.
4. The player who finds the most objects wins the game.

Next Time
- Instead of restricting your search to a particular category, include anything that relates to the category. For example, if the category is cars, include tires, maps, roads, other modes of transportation, a radio, and so on.

Ages: 7 to 12 years

Peek a Boo

Can your child guess what she sees through the peephole?

Values
- Curiosity

Skills
- Perception

Materials
- Magazine

How to Play
1. Ask for an old magazine you can tear up, or bring one with you.
2. Look for an interesting picture without letting your child see it.
3. Poke a hole in the previous page and fold back the edges of the hole so your child can see only a little bit of the picture.
4. Let him look through the peephole and try to guess what the picture is.
5. Give him clues if he gets stuck.
6. Take turns poking holes and guessing.

Next Time
- If you don't want to poke holes in the magazine, use a sheet of paper with a hole in it to cover the picture.

Ages: 4 to 8 years

Pull Out a Story

Your child can make up a story about anything if he has a good imagination.

Values
- Resourcefulness

Skills
- Creativity and Imagination
- Language and Vocabulary

Materials
- Objects nearby

How to Play
1. Have your child choose an object nearby that interests him, such as a garbage truck, neon light, cat, and so on.
2. Have him make up a story about the object.
3. Have him find another object and continue the story using the new object.
4. Have him continue until his story is over or he runs out of objects.

Next Time
- Imagine other objects to add to your child's story and name them for him. Have him include each object in the next part of his story.

Ages: 6 to 10 years

Same and Different

How many similarities can your child find between two objects? How many differences?

Values
- Environmental Awareness

Skills
- Critical Thinking

Materials Needed
- Variety of objects

How to Play
1. While you're waiting in line, select two objects.
2. Have your child study the objects and identify one thing they have in common.
3. Then have her describe one way in which they're different.
4. Count the number of similarities and differences until she runs out of comparisons.

Next Time
- Choose three objects to compare.

Story Seer

Can your child guess what's going to happen on the next page of his book? Maybe he has ESP!

Values
- Teamwork

Skills
- Language and Vocabulary

Materials
- Picture book or storybook

How to Play
1. Choose an unfamiliar picture book or storybook.
2. Read the first page together and look at the picture.
3. Have your child try to guess what's going to happen on the next page.
4. Read the next page and see how accurate his prediction was.
5. Continue through the story until it's finished.

Next Time
- Read the first few pages of a book and have your child try to guess what's going to happen at the end. Then finish reading the story and find out if he was right.

Trip to the Factory

What would it be like for your child to take a trip inside a place where interesting things are made?

Values
- Resourcefulness

Skills
- Critical Thinking

Materials
- Object nearby

How to Play
1. Have your child choose an object nearby, such as a telephone, article of clothing, food item, toy, and so on.
2. Have her imagine what the factory is like where the object is made.
3. Have her take an imaginary tour of the factory. Help her get started, if necessary.
4. Talk about what she "sees," including a description of how the object is made.

Next Time
- Take your child on a trip to an interesting place such as another country, inside a building, on a balloon ride, into the city, into the country, inside a factory, and so on.

Ages: 5 to 10 years

Truth Be Told

Does your child know the truth about his family and friends?

Values

- Importance of Family

Skills

- Perception
- Social Interaction

Materials

- Nothing

How to Play

1. Make a statement about yourself, such as, "My favorite color is red," "I like lima beans," "I want to try skydiving," and so on.
2. Ask your child if he thinks the statement is true or false.
3. Answer him truthfully and ask him why he thought it was true or false.
4. Take turns making true or false statements and having the other person guess.

Next Time

- Invite other family members and friends to join the game.

Ages: 6 to 12 years

What Can You Tell?

Can your child tell something about a person by looking inside his or her shopping cart?

Values

- Environmental Awareness

Skills

- Critical Thinking
- Curiosity

Materials

- Nothing

How to Play

1. While you and your child are waiting in line at the grocery store, notice the contents of another customer's shopping cart.
2. Have your child try to guess what that person will be making for dinner.
3. Have your child try to guess how many people are in the person's family and their ages.

Next Time

- Talk about what else you can determine about a person by noticing his or her purchases. For example, is the person a vegetarian or a meat eater? Does he or she have a sweet tooth? Is the person a bargain hunter?

"I see something brown with green things on it."
Tree !

Ages: 4 to 7 years

What Do I See?

Does your child see what you see? What does it look like?

Values
- Environmental Awareness

Skills
- Language and Vocabulary

Materials
- Objects nearby

How to Play
1. Find something nearby that you'd like to describe.
2. Describe the object and have your child guess what it is.
3. Give her clues until she figures it out.
4. Take turns describing objects and guessing what they are.

Next Time
- Describe an object that isn't visible and see if your child can guess what it is.

Ages: 7 to 12 years

What's Your Problem?

Two heads are better than one when it comes to solving a problem.

Values
- Helping Others

Skills
- Problem Solving

Materials
- Nothing

How to Play
1. Think of a mild problem you're having, such as, "I can't get my work done," "I don't know what to make for dinner," "I'm worried about a speech I have to give," and so on.
2. Explain your problem in detail. Tell your child what's bothering you, what you're stuck on, or what you need help with.
3. Let her offer some solutions, and see which ones might work.
4. Let your child share a problem with you. Brainstorm ideas that might help her.

Next Time
- Imagine some other problems and see if you can solve them together.

Chapter Thirteen

Walking Time!

Ages: 6 to 10 years

Bird Watching

Your child sees birds in the sky all the time, but does he know their names?

Values
- Environmental Awareness
- Respect for Nature

Skills
- Classification

Materials
- Bird identification book
- Binoculars
- Notebook and pencil

How to Play
1. Get a bird identification book from the library or bookstore.
2. As you go on your walk, watch for birds together.
3. When you spot one, share the binoculars and take a good look at the bird.
4. Have your child describe the bird and try to identify it by looking in the book.
5. Write down the name of bird or have your child draw a picture of it in his notebook.
6. Look for more birds to add to the notebook.

Next Time
- Search for other animals (cows, horses, dogs, cats, and so on) and have your child try to identify them. Use reference books, if necessary.

Ages: 6 to 12 years

Blind Walk

How much does your child trust you? Find out on a blind walk.

Values
- Teamwork

Skills
- Following Directions

Materials
- Blindfold

How to Play
1. Find a safe area to walk.
2. Blindfold your child or have him close his eyes—no peeking.
3. Start the walk by holding his hand and leading him down the path. Make sure he's safe so he will trust you.
4. Give him verbal instructions so he can avoid obstacles such as low branches, dips in the path, and so on.
5. Have him feel some of the plants and leaves along the way.
6. Have him talk about what he experiences with his other senses.
7. When he's ready, let go of his hand and lead him only with your voice.

Next Time
- Take a blind walk through the mall, grocery store, a strange neighborhood, your house, and so on.

Ages: 5 to 12 years

Cleanup Crew

Organize your cleanup crew to clean up the park or neighborhood.

Values
- Achievement/Success
- Respect for Nature

Skills
- Recycling

Materials
- Bag
- Sponge
- Soap and water

How to Play
1. While you're out on your walk, find an area that needs a cleanup, such as a park bench, garden, field, fence, and so on.
2. Have your child think about how she might improve the area with soap and water, litter removal, and so on.
3. Set a date to return to the spot.
4. Gather the supplies and make the improvements together.
5. Admire your work.
6. Repeat each week.

Next Time
- Look around your house and see what needs cleaning up.

Ages: 3 to 6 years

Color Coded

Can your child find all the colors of the rainbow right under his nose?

Values
- Environmental Awareness

Skills
- Classification

Materials
- Paper and pencil

How to Play
1. Have your child choose a color before he begins the walk. You do the same.
2. See how many objects you can find in your colors. For example, if your child chooses red, he might see a flower, ladybug, and so on.
3. Write down what you find.
4. See who finds the most objects in his or her color.

Next Time
- Have your child choose a shape, number, or letter of the alphabet and see how many he can find on your walk.

Ages: 6 to 10 years

Count Down

Count the objects you see as you go along on your walk.

Values
- Environmental Awareness

Skills
- Math

Materials
- Nothing

How to Play
1. As you begin your walk, think of one object you hope to find along the way, such as an oak tree, a bluebird, or a cow.
2. After you have found the object, think of two objects to find, such as two cats, two blue cars, or two men with hats.
3. Continue in this manner until you reach the number ten.

Next Time
- As you go on your walk, find something whose name begins with the letter *a* and continue through the rest of the alphabet.

Ages: 3 to 8 years

Did You Hear That?

Can your child identify the sounds he hears in the environment?

Values
- Environmental Awareness

Skills
- Perception

Materials
- Paper and pencils

How to Play
1. As you go on your walk, stop every few minutes and listen to the sounds around you.
2. See if you and your child can separately identify five sounds. Each of you write them down, but don't reveal your list.
3. Continue walking, listening, and writing down what you hear.
4. When you're finished walking, check your lists and see if they match.
5. See if you missed any sounds the other person heard.

Next Time
- Close your eyes as you're walking. When you hear a particular sound, open your eyes and see if you can locate the source of the sound.

Ages: 3 to 8 years

Five Senses

Have your child explore her senses as she explores the environment.

Values
- Environmental Awareness

Skills
- Perception

Materials
- Nothing

How to Play
1. As you're out walking, have your child stop what she's doing and check on her five senses.
2. Discuss what she sees, hears, smells, tastes, and feels.
3. See if things change each time she stops to check her senses.

Next Time
- See if you and your child are sensing the same things.

Ages: 7 to 12 years

Gizmos

Can your child explain some of the oddities of nature?

Values
- Resourcefulness

Skills
- Critical Thinking

Materials
- Unusual things in nature

How to Play
1. As you take your walk, have your child look for unusual things in nature, such as an oddly shaped rock, a strange plant, an interesting constellation, and so on.
2. Have her try to explain the natural phenomena. She might say the objects were created by forces of nature, brought to Earth by aliens, dropped from outer space, and so on.
3. Help her explain the circumstances, if possible.
4. Find other objects and have your child try to explain their origins, purposes, and so on.

Next Time
- Have your child think of things she could do with the objects.
- Make up stories about the objects.

Ages: 6 to 10 years

Neighborhood Map

Walk around different areas in your neighborhood and make some new discoveries.

Values
- Environmental Awareness

Skills
- Gross Motor
- Map Reading

Materials
- Map of the neighborhood
- Paper and pencil
- Marker or highlighter

How to Play
1. Find a map of your neighborhood or make one.
2. Take a walk in one area of your neighborhood and remember the streets you take.
3. When you return home, have your child mark or highlight the areas where you walked on the map.
4. Plan your next walk in a new part of the neighborhood.
5. See how much new territory you can cover during each walk.

Next Time
- See if your child can find the way home without the map.

Ages: 3 to 8 years

See a Shape

Your child can see shapes all around him if he looks carefully.

Values
- Environmental Awareness

Skills
- Classification

Materials
- Nothing

How to Play
1. Have your child choose a shape such as a circle, square, triangle, rectangle, and so on.
2. See how many objects of that shape he can find while you're out on your walk.
3. When he finds ten, have him choose a new shape and see if he can find ten objects of that shape.

Next Time
- See how many different types of circles your child can find, such as big, moving, bright, flowered, every color of the rainbow, and so on.

Ages: 6 to 10 years

Show the Way

Use hand signals to set the course for your walk.

Values

- Teamwork

Skills

- Following Directions

Materials

- None

How to Play

1. Before you begin your walk, make up some hand signals with your child. For example, you might hold your hand up to mean "stop," wave your hand forward to mean "go," turn your hand left or right to signal "turn left" or "turn right," move your hand up and down to mean "take the steps," incline your hand downward to mean "walk down the hill," incline your hand upward to mean "climb," and so on.
2. Use the hand signals as you walk to show your child the route.

Next Time

- Have your child choose a walking route (without revealing it to you) and show you the way using hand signals.

Ages: 6 to 10 years

Steady Hands

Can your child walk and talk and keep a stick steady all at the same time?

Values
- Perseverance

Materials
- Stick

Skills
- Coordination/Balance
- Fine Motor
- Gross Motor

How to Play
1. Find a stick your child can use to balance.
2. Have her try to balance the stick on her palm.
3. Have her try to walk and keep the stick balanced.
4. Have her try to balance it while keeping her eyes closed.

Next Time
- Have your child walk with her eyes closed and gently swing the stick back and forth in front of her to guide her.

Ages: 6 to 10 years

Time Traveler

How would your child describe her life to someone who lived long ago?

Values
- Positive Attitude

Skills
- Communication
- Critical Thinking

Materials Needed
- Nothing

How to Play
1. Pretend you're a visitor from the past. Ask your child to describe what's so great about living today.
2. If she has trouble thinking of examples, ask her specific questions such as "What's the best food?" "What's the best tool?" "What's the best invention?" "What's the best entertainment?" and so on.

Next Time
- Tell your child to pretend she lives in another time period. Ask her what's so great about that time.

Ages: 3 to 8 years

Wacky Walk

You'll have fun doing a wacky walk with your child!

Values
- Sense of Humor

Skills
- Creativity and Imagination
- Gross Motor

Materials
- Nothing

How to Play
1. While you're taking your walk, have your child think of a funny way to walk, such as with wiggly legs, stiff-legged, bowlegged, limping, dragging a foot, pigeon-toed, splayfooted, and so on.
2. Have him change his wacky walk every few minutes.

Next Time
- Have your child add wacky arm movements to the wacky walk.
- Have him add other wacky movements to the wacky walk.
- Play Follow the Leader while doing a wacky walk.

Ages: 4 to 8 years

Walk Backward

Have your child see things in reverse by walking backward.

Values
- Resourcefulness

Skills
- Gross Motor
- Perception

Materials
- Nothing

How to Play
1. Choose a safe path to walk along.
2. Have your child walk backward and see how well he does.
3. Take a turn yourself.
4. Think of funny steps to add to your backward walk.

Next Time
- While you're walking backward, do others things backward such as talk backward, recite the alphabet backward, and so on.

Index

C

D

E

F

G

H

I

J

K

L

M

N

T

W

Y